AIRLINE SERVICE ENGLISH & TOURISM ENGLISH

항공관광영어

고선희 박정민 공저

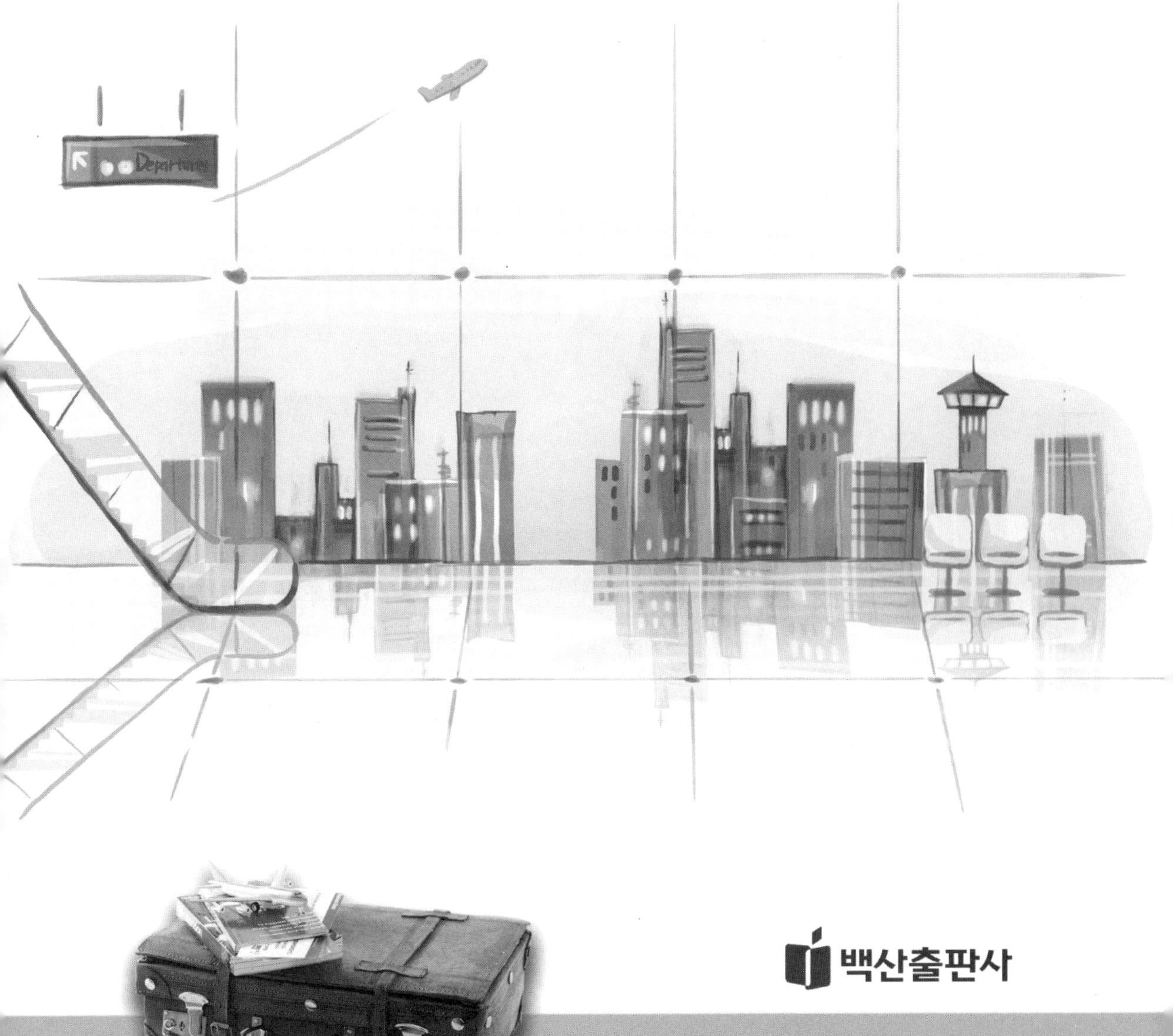

백산출판사

PREFACE

21세기 운송수단의 비약적 발전으로 글로벌 관광시대가 도래하면서 항공운송산업은 눈부시게 발전하여 왔다. 대형 항공사를 비롯하여 2005년 한성항공을 시초로 우리나라에서도 중·소형 항공기를 이용한 LCC가 시장 진입하게 됨에 따라 많은 항공 관련학과가 신설되었고, 항공운송산업 종사자의 수요는 더 많아지게 되었다.

이에 항공서비스와 관광서비스에 종사하게 될 학생들에게 적시적소에 사용가능한 항공관광영어의 필요성이 그 어느 때보다 대두되었기에 본 저서를 집필하게 되었다.

이 책은 크게 PART 1. AIRLINE SERVICE ENGLISH과 PART 2. TOURISM ENGLISH로 구성되어 있으며 PART 3에서는 기본적인 READING SKILL의 향상과 한국의 문화를 외국인에게 알리는 데 도움을 주고자 INSIDE KOREA로 구성하였고 PART 4에서는 LISTING SKILL의 향상을 위하여 DICTATION을 할 수 있게 구성하여 놓았다. 그 외 기본영어회화에 반드시 필요한 표현 Useful Expressions와 항공서비스에 필요한 Today's Tip 표현을 각 CHAPTER마다 삽입하였다.

먼저 AIRLINE SERVICE ENGLISH는 항공기 탑승 전에 필요한 표현들을 〈CHAPTER 1 ~ CHAPTER 4〉까지 정리하였으며 항공기 탑승 후의 표현들은 서비스 제공순서에 준하여 〈CHAPTER 5 ~ CHAPTER 11〉까지 정리하였다. 각 CHAPTER마다 삽입된 Useful Expressions는 날씨, 건강, 나이, 생일, 개인경험, 키, 몸무게, 생김새, 성격, 외모 묘사하기 등에 관한 표현들을 다양하게 제시하여 기초생활회화에 활용할 수 있도록 하였다.

TOURISM ENGLISH는 호텔에서 필요한 상황들을 접점 순으로 나열하여 Reservation부터 Check Out까지 정리하여, 추후 호텔근무 시 또는 호텔이용 시 활용할 수 있도록 하였다.

마지막으로 본서의 활용을 위하여 제작된 MP3를 통하여 정확한 발음, 억양, 속도 등을 따라하면서 반복해서 학습해 본다면 영어실력 향상에 많은 발전이 있을 것이라 기대된다.

책 출판을 위해 많은 도움을 주신 백산출판사 진욱상 사장님께 진심으로 감사의 마음을 전하며, 감수에 도움을 주신 JANNET 교수님과 편집부 직원들께 깊은 감사를 드린다.

2009. 12.

고선희 · 박정민

CONTENTS

PART 1 AIRLINE SERVICE ENGLISH

PART 2 TOURISM ENGLISH

PART 3 INSIDE KOREA

PART 4 DICTATION

PART 1

AIRLINE SERVICE ENGLISH

Dialogue 1

CHAPTER 1
RESERVATION

1

C : Reservation Clerk, P : Passenger

C : Asiana Airlines. Can I help you?

P : I want to make a reservation to Manila the day after tomorrow.

C : Yes, Ma'am. What time would you like to fly?

P : Is there a flight early in the morning?

C : Yes, there is. We have a flight at 8 a.m.

P : I'll take that.

C : O.K. May I have your name, please?

P : Lucy Lee.

C : May I have your phone number, please?

P : The number is 031-205-6732.

C : O.K. Your reservation has been made for flight 701 leaving for Manila on Aug. 13, Sunday at 7 a.m. Your reservation number is C67576. Thank you for calling Asiana Airlines.

P : Thank you Bye.

Dialogue 2

C : Good morning. Ha-na Travel agency.
This is Ms. Park speaking.
How May I help you?

P : Good morning. I'm planning a trip to New York this winter and was wondering if you could give me some information on the airfare.

C : Sure. When do you want to travel?

P : Anytime on Jan. 1st. How much is a round-trip ticket to New York?

C : Do you have any airline you prefer?

P : Not really.

C : Well, Fly Airline Offers 1,100,000 won for a round-trip ticket to JFK. It's a direct flight.

P : Wow, that's pretty expensive. Do you have any lower rates?

C : Well, The cheapest one we have is one million won, World Airline.

P : That sounds better.

Dialogue 3

2

C : Good afternoon. May I help you?

P : Do you have a flight from Incheon to LA on May 5th?

C : When would you like to leave?

P : In the afternoon May 5th.

C : You have to change another flight. That one is booked.

P : When is the next flight?

C : How about the 8 p.m. flight, ma'am?

P : 8 o'clock in the evening? That's available. I'll take that one.

C : Please be sure to check-in at the airport at least two hours before your flight time.

Dialogue 4

C : But it's not a direct flight. It stops over in Tokyo.

P : That doesn't matter. How many flights does it have daily?

C : They have two flights daily, one at 3:30 p.m. and another at 8:00 p.m.

P : I'd better take the earlier one. When does it arrive in New York?

C : It arrives in New York at 4:40 p.m. on the same day. When would you like to return?

P : Can I leave it open?

C : Of course, you can. Are you a student?

P : Yes. My sister and I are both students.

C : In that case, I Can give you a student discount. That's 20% off. So that'll be 800,000 won for each.

P : Great! That's even better. Could you book me on that?

Dialogue 5

C : World Airline reservation. How can I help you?

P : Hi, I'd like to confirm my reservation.

C : Can I have your last name, please?

P : My last name is Kim and my first name is Mi-Ae. I'm travelling with my brother.

C : Could you tell me the date you leave?

P : Oh, I have the reservation number. Would it be any help?

C : Oh, sure. Please go ahead.

P : It's CBCD2F.

Useful Expressions

*현재 날씨에 관해 말하기

What's the weather doing now? 지금 날씨가 어때?
How's the weather now?

It's	raining.	비가 와요.
	drizzling.	가랑비가 와요.
	pouring.	폭우가 와요.
	snowing.	눈이 내려요.
	blowing.	바람이 불어요.
	shining.	해가 쨍쨍해요.
	freezing.	얼어 죽겠어요.
	hailing.	우박이 와요.
	sleeting.	진눈깨비가 와요.

*몸이 아프다고 말하기

I have		
	a backache.	등이 아파요.
	a bloody nose.	코피가 나요.
	a cold.	감기에 걸렸어요.
	a cough.	기침이 나요.
	a fever.	열이 나요.
	a headache.	머리가 아파요.
	an earache.	귀가 아파요.
	an infection.	감염이 됐어요.
	an insect bite.	벌레에 물렸어요.
	a rash.	발진이 일어났어요.
	a runny nose.	콧물이 나와요.
	a sore throat.	목안이 아파요.
	a stiff neck.	목이 뻣뻣해요.
	a stomachache.	배가 아파요.
	a sunburn.	햇볕에 탔어요.
	a toothache.	이가 아파요.
	laryngitis.	후두염에 걸렸어요.

I have	the hiccups.	딸꾹질이 나와요.
	the chills.	몸이 으슬으슬 떨려요.
I feel	faint.	쓰러질 것 같아요.
	dizzy.	어지러워요.
	nauseous.	속이 메스꺼워요.
	bloated.	몸이 부은 것 같아요.

＊몸은 괜찮은지 / 회복되기를 바란다고 말하기

Are you okay?	너 괜찮니?
Are you alright?	괜찮아요?
What's the matter?	무슨 일이에요?
What's the problem?	무슨 문제가 있나요?
What's wrong?	뭐가 잘못되었나요?
I'm sorry you're not feeling well.	몸이 별로 안 좋다니 안됐어요.
I hope you feel better soon.	빨리 낫길 바라요.
I hope you get better soon.	곧 회복되길 바라요.

Dialogue 1

3 P : Hello, Is this the Ana Airlines ticket office?

C : Yes, it is. May I help you?

P : I need to confirm my reservation to Tokyo.

C : O.K., sir. Your name, please?

P : Daniel Jackson.

C : Your reservation is confirmed in economy class. Your departure time is 7:30 a.m.

P : Is that direct flight?

C : Sure.

P : When can I receive the ticket?

C : You can receive your ticket tomorrow through e-mail.

P : Can I send my payment on line or by credit card?

C : Either is fine.

P : What credit cards do you accept?

C : Any major credit card will be fine.

P : Very well. Thank you.

Dialogue 2

C : Would you hold the line for a second?

P : Yes.

C : Thank you for waiting, Miss Kim. You're flying to New York on Flight 179, economy class, leaving at 3:30 p.m. on Jan. 1st. Right?

P : Correct.

C : OK, your reservation is confirmed. Your confirmation number is the same as your reservation number.

P : Is that all?

C : One more thing. Will you please check in two hours prior to the departure time?

P : OK, I will. But why is that?

C : You have to check in for the flight and go through immigration. It takes about that time.

P : I see. Thanks for your help.

C : Thank you for calling. Have a nice trip!

Dialogue 3

C : Good morning. Korean Airlines reservation. Can I help you?

P : I'd like to cancel my reservation on flight 397 for the 13 of next month.

C : Oh, I see. Can I have your name, please?

P : Daniel Lee.

C : One moment please, Mr. Lee.

(Pause)

Thank you for waiting, sir. Now your reservation is cancelled. Do you want to make a new schedule?

P : No, I haven't fixed my schedule yet.

C : All right, sir. Thank you for calling.

Please, call us again whenever you want to make a new reservation. Good-bye, sir.

Useful Expressions

*일기 예보에 관해 말하기

What's the weather report? 일기 예보가 어때?
What's the weather forecast?

There's going to be	lightning.	번개가 칠 거래.
	a snowstorm.	눈보라가 칠 거래.
	a hurricane / a typhoon.	태풍이 온대.
	a thunder storm.	뇌우가 있을 거래.
	a flood.	홍수가 날 거래.
	a shower.	소나기가 올 거래.

*날씨에 관해 말하기

What's the weather like in Seoul? 서울의 날씨는 어때요?
How's the weather in New York? 뉴욕의 날씨는 어때요?

It's	chilly.	쌀쌀해요.
	clear.	맑아요.
	cold.	추워요.
	cool.	서늘해요.
	dry.	건조해요.
	hot.	더워요.
	humid.	습도가 높아요.
	mild.	온화해요.
	warm.	따뜻해요.
	wet.	비가 자주 와요.

What was the weather like yesterday? 어제 날씨는 어땠죠?
How was the weather during your trip? 여행하는 동안 날씨는 어땠어요?

It was	nice.	좋았어요.
	lovely.	멋졌어요.
	wonderful.	굉장히 좋았어요.
	terrible.	형편없었어요.
	awful.	끔찍했어요.
	nasty.	험악했어요.

*나이에 관해서 묻고 답하기

How old	are	you?
		they?
	is	she?
		he?

What's	your	age?
	her	
	his	

You don't look your age.

You look	younger	than your age.
	older	

You look	young	for your age.
	old	

Dialogue 1

4

A : Airline counter

P : Passenger

A : Good afternoon, ma'am. What can I help you with?

P : I'd like to buy an air ticket to LA.

A : Would you like one way or round trip?

P : I want a round trip ticket, please.

A : What flight do you want to take?

P : I'll take the earliest flight possible.

Dialogue 2

A : Good morning. How may I help you?

P : Yes, I made a reservation for a flight to Tokyo on Saturday.

A : May I have your name, ma'am?

P : My name is Jannet smith.

A : You are going to Tokyo OZ 102, economy class, aren't you?
It is $1050 for the round trip, Ms. Smith.

P : What kind of card do you accept?

A : We accept all kinds of credit cards.

P : Do you accept Visa card, too?

A : Sure. May I have your card and passport?

P : Here you are.

A : Would you please sign here, Ms. Smith?

P : Sure.

A : Do you need anything else?

P : No, that's all.

Today's Tip

Fare / fee / price

fare는 주로 교통기관의 요금, fee는 각종 수수료나 전문적인 일에 대한 대가로 지불되는 요금이고, price는 가장 일반적으로 쓰이며 주로 상품에 지불되는 금액을 나타낼 때 사용한다.

A : How much is the bus fare?
B : It's $1.50.
A : I have two one-dollar bills.
B : Sorry. You need to have the exact change.
A : 버스 요금이 얼마죠?
B : 1달러 50센트입니다.
A : 1달러짜리 지폐 두 장이 있는데요.
B : 죄송합니다. 정확하게 잔돈으로 준비하셔야 돼요.

A : I heard you recently moved. How do you like your new place?
B : Couldn't be better, except that I paid one month's rent for the broker fee.
A : 이사했다면서. 새 집은 맘에 들어?
B : 최고야. 한 달치 세를 중개수수료로 낸 것만 빼고는.

A : Is this real? $2.99 for a pair of shoes?
B : This is a special price. Get it now, or you'll regret it.
A : 이거 정말이에요? 신발 한 켤레에 $2.99밖에 안 해요?
B : 특별가예요. 지금 사지 않으면 후회하실 거예요.

Today's Tip

Luggage & Baggage

짐(가방), 수화물이란 뜻을 가진 단어 중에서 luggage와 baggage는 항상 집합명사로 쓰이기 때문에 복수형을 만들 수가 없습니다. 대신에 개수를 셀 때에는 a piece of를 써서 a piece of luggage(baggage), two pieces of luggage(baggage)라고 합니다.

A : I'd like to check my luggage.
B : Sure. How many pieces of luggage do you have?
A : Just one.
A : 짐을 부치려고 하는데요.
B : 네, 짐이 몇 개나 되시죠?
A : 하나밖에 없어요.

A : What is your baggage allowance?
B : We allow only two pieces of baggage per person.
A : What if someone has more?
B : If it exceeds the limit, you have to pay extra charge.
A : 수화물 제한이 어떻게 되나요?
B : 일인당 두 개의 짐만 부칠 수 있습니다.
A : 짐이 더 많으면요?
B : 만약 제한을 초과하면 추가 요금을 내셔야 합니다.

A : Excuse me. My luggage hasn't come out.
B : Do you have your baggage checks?
A : 실례합니다. 제 짐이 나오지 않았는데요.
B : 수화물 표를 가지고 계신가요?

Dialogue 1

5

A : Airline agent

P : Passenger

A : Good evening, sir. May I see your ticket and passport?

P : Here you are.

A : Do you have any baggage to check in?

P : Yes. I have two suitcases and one golf club bag.

A : Would you put your baggage on the scale?

P : O.K. Can you put a fragile tag on my suitcases?

A : All right. Here are your baggage claim tags and boarding pass, sir. Have a nice flight!

P : Thanks a lot.

Dialogue 2

A : Good morning. Can I have your ticket and passport, please?

P : Here you are.

A : Would you like an aisle seat or window seat?

P : I prefer an aisle seat please.

I want to go to lavatory without disturbing another passenger during the flight.

A : O.K. I see.

Do you have any baggage to check in?

P : Yes. one.

A : Could you put your baggage on the scale, please?

P : All right.

A : Here are your boarding pass and baggage claim tag.

Your seat is 35c and the boarding Gate is 27.

P : Thank you so much.

A : You're welcome. Enjoy your trip.

Dialogue 3

6 A : Hello. Are you flying to San Francisco today?

P : Yes, I have my e-ticket.

A : Great. I need to see your passport as well.

P : Here you are.

A : I'll check.

Great. Here you are.

P : Would I be able to get an aisle seat?

A : Sure.

P : Thanks.

A : Are you just checking these bags?

P : Yes, I'll take my backpack as my carry-on.

A : Anything fragile in your bags?

P : No.

A : Okay. Here is your boarding pass. Be at the gate one hour prior to boarding time.

Dialogue 4

A : Would you prefer a window or an aisle seat?

P : Which one is better?

A : That depends. Some people like to look at the clouds during the flight. But, the window seats are harder to get in and out of.

P : I'll take the aisle, then.

Dialogue 5

P : Do I check in here for World Airline Flight 179 to New York?

A : Yes. Do you already have your tickets?

P : Yes. Here you are.

A : Thank you. May I see your passports, too?

P : Sure. Can I have a window seat, please?

A : Let's see. Good. We have seat 12H and 12K. Do you have any luggage to check in?

P : Yes, we have two suitcases and one carry-on.

A : Is your name and address on your bag. ma'am?

P : Yes, it is.

A : Can you put your luggage up here, please?

P : OK.

Dialogue 6

7 A : Here are your tickets and your boarding passes. Flight 272 to Seattle. Seat 12H and 12K. It departs from Gate 11 at 3:20. Enjoy your flight!

P1 : Thank you. Could you tell me where departure gate 11 is, please?

A : Yes. Just take the escalator up to the next level and turn right. All the gates are upstairs.

P2 : Thanks.

P1 : Is it possible to buy souvenirs and gifts here?

A : Yes. Go to level 2. Look for the duty-free shop in the departure area. It's near the telephones. You can't miss it. You'll find lots of famous brands there.

P2 : Thanks for the help.

Dialogue 7

Getting on board

Announcement : Passengers for Seattle, may I have your attention. please? World Airline's Flight 272 to Seattle, scheduled to depart at 3:30, has been delayed due to late arrival from Tokyo. Flight 272 will now depart at 3:50 from Gate 11. Boarding will begin in 15 minutes.

Dialogue 8

Announcement : Good afternoon. World Airline Flight 179 departing at 3:50 for JFK Airport in New York City is now preboarding at Gate 11. Passengers with small children or who require special help in boarding, please proceed to Gate 11, now. The Flight is 20 minutes behind schedule and will depart at 3:50 p.m. now. Sorry for the delay. Next, all those passengers in rows 39 through 56, please board.

(on the plane)

C : Good afternoon, ma'am. What's your seat number?
P : Uh, it's 12K.
C : That's on the left side of the airplane. It's by the window.
P : Thank you.

Useful Expressions

*생일에 관해서 묻고 답하기

When were you born?
When is your birthday?
what is your date of birth?
What date is your birthday?

I was born on May 14, 1980.
It's in August.
It's May 10th.
It's the third of June.

*개인적인 경험에 관해서 물어보기

How long	have	you	been	living in this town?
		we		dating?
		they		studying English?
	has	he		attending this school?
		she		playing the piano?

I've been studying English for 10 years.

How long has it been since	you saw Mary?
	he called you?
	they broke up?

It has been two weeks.

*키에 관해서 묻고 답하기

How tall	are	you?
	is	she?
		he?
		Maria?

I'm	152cm.
	five feet four inches tall.
	five two.

I'm	a little	short.
	fairly	tall.
	kind of	
	pretty	
	rather	

I'm	medium	height.
	average	tall.

*머리 스타일에 관해서 묻고 답하기

What's	your his her	hair like?

It's	straight. wavy. curly.

It's	long. short. medium length. shoulder length.

It's	blond. black. gray. red.

CHAPTER 5
BOARDING

Dialogue 1

8

C : Cabin Attendant

P : Passenger

C : Good morning, sir. Welcome aboard.

P : Good morning. Where is 43G.

C : Please take the other aisle.

Your seat is in the back of the cabin.

P : Thanks.

C : You're welcome, sir.

Dialogue 2

P : Excuse me. Where is my seat?

C : It's over there 33B, your seat is in the middle of the cabin on your right.

P : Thank you.

C : Anytime, ma'am. Have a nice flight.

Dialogue 3

P : Excuse me. miss.

Where can I put my bag? It's too big. And I can't find any room for it.

C : Would you like me to keep your bag in the coatroom?

P : Please. Thank you.

C : It's my pleasure.

C : Excuse me, ma'am. Is this your bag?

P : Yes, why?

C : I'm sorry. ma'am.

Would you please put it under the seat in front of you.

We must keep the aisle clear.

P : All right.

C : Thank you very much.

C : Excuse me, sir.

Would you mind putting it under the seat?

It might fall during turbulence.

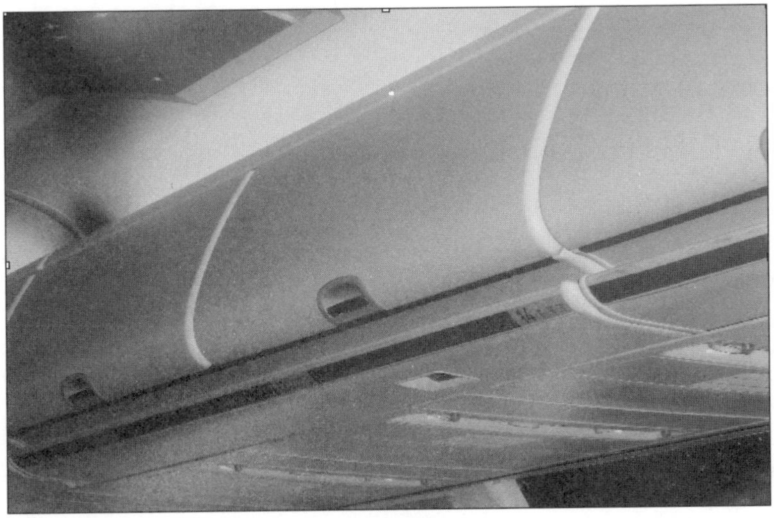

Overhead bin

Dialogue 4

9 C : Good morning. ma'am.

May I see your boarding pass, please?

P : Here you are.

C : Your seat number is 37B. It's on your right side.

May I help you with your bag?

P : Here you are.

C : Thank you.

C : Excuse me. ma'am. May I help you?

P : No. I'm just stretching.

C : Would you please take your seat during boarding?

P : Okay, I'll sit.

C : Thank you, ma'am.

C : Excuse me, sir. May I help you?

P : No. I'm looking around.

C : Would you please step aside to let these people through?

P : Okay, I'll sit.

C : Thank you, sir.

입양되는 아기와 함께한 승무원

Dialogue 5

C : Good morning, ma'am. May I help you with your bags?

P : Yes, please. Oh, thank you, sir.

C : Come this way, please. This is your seat.

Please keep this bag in the overhead bin.

P : May I have some water?

C : I will get it for you after everyone has boarded. ma'am.

(Pause)

Here's your water, ma'am.

P : Thank you.

Useful Expressions

*몸무게에 관해서 묻고 답하기

How much do you weigh?

What do you weigh?

I've	gained / put on	some / a little / a bit of / a lot of	weight.
		six	kilograms.

I've	lost	some	weight.
	cut down	a little	
		a bit of	
		a lot of	
		six	kilograms.

I've	slimmed down	some.
		a little.
		a bit.

*얼굴 특징에 관해서 말하기

She has pale	skin.	
	light	
	dark	
	suntanned.	

She has	blue	eyes.
	gray	
	brown	

She has	thick	eyebrows.
	thin	

He has	a beard.
	mustache.
	scar.
	beauty mark.

She has	freckles.
	dimples.
	sideburns.

*생김새에 관해서 묻고 답하기

What	do	you	look like?
		they	
	does	she	
		he	

I	am	handsome.
She	is	beautiful.
He		good-looking.
They	are	attractive.

I	am	heavy.
She	is	slender.
He		thin.
They	are	askinny.

Dialogue 1

10

P1 : Excuse me, miss. Somebody is sitting on my seat.

C : May I see your boarding pass, please?

Thank you.

(to P2) Excuse me, sir.

May I see your boarding pass, please?

Thank you, sir.

I'm sorry but I'm afraid you might be in the wrong seat.

Your seat is over there.

Would you please change seats?

I'll help you with your bags.

P2 : Oh, all right.

C : (to P1) Thank you for waiting, sir.

Dialogue 2

P : Do you have any empty seats in front of the cabin

C : Would you please wait until everyone has boarded. sir?
I'll check it for you later.
(Pause)

C : We have some empty seats in the front of the cabin.
(Move to the front seat)
Would you like to sit there?

P : Can I move in back of the cabin. I think there are empty seats.

C : Would you please wait until everyone has boarded. sir?
Let me check it for you later.
(Pause)

C : I'm sorry.
All the seats are occupied today.

Dialogue 3

11 P1 : Miss, there's someone in my seat.

C : (to both)

May I see your boarding pass, please?

Thank you

I'm afraid there was a mistake in the arrangement of seats.

(to P1)

Come this way please.

Would you please wait here?

I will check it right away.

Just a moment, please.

(to P1)

Thank you for waiting sir. Your seat is rearranged.

This way, please.

Here you are.

I'm sorry for the inconvenience.

Dialogue 4

P : Excuse me, my son and I were assigned separate seats.
Do you have any empty seats together?

C : Oh, I'll check. We have some seats in the middle of the cabin. Would that be alright?

P : That's good. thank you.

C : May I help you with your bags?

P : No, thank you. That's alright.

C : Come this way, please.
Have a pleasant flight.

P : Excuse me, my wife and I were assigned separate seats.
Do you have any empty seats together?

C : I'm sorry, sir. But after take-off, I'll come back and let you know.

(after take off)

I'm sorry, sir. But all the seats are occupied today.

Is there anything else I can do for you?

P : Oh, No. Thank you. that's all.

Dialogue 5

P : My colleagues are sitting over there, and we want to sit together.

Can I change my seat?

C : I'll check after everyone has boarded and let you know.

(after boarding)

Thanks for waiting, I have found some seats for you.

Come this way please.

Useful Expressions

*누구와 닮았는지 묻고 답하기

Who do you look like?
Do you look like your father or mother?

닮았을 때

I look [a lot / a little / more] like my grandmother. / grandfather.

I look the same as my [mother. / father.]

I'm [an identical / a fraternal] twin.

닮지 않았을 때

I don't look like my sister. / brother.

My sister / brother and I look different from each other.

*외모가 어떻게 보이는지 물어보기

How do I / we / they look?
How does she / he look?

You / We / They look great. / gorgeous. / wonderful.

She / He looks pale. / tired. / nervous.

CHAPTER 7
GROUND SERVICE

Dialogue 1

12

Newspaper service

C : Would you like to read a newspaper, sir?

P : I'll have the Cho-sun Il-bo.

C : Sure. Here you are.

C : Would you care for a newspaper, ma'am?

P : Do you have Newsweek?

C : I'm sorry, ma'am.

Newsweek is not available in this flight.

Would you like the Korea Times, instead?

Earphone service

C : Here are your earphones, sir.

P : Thank you

When are you going to show the movie?

C : We'll be showing the movie in about 2 hours.

Dialogue 2

Mother with a baby

C : We prepared some baby items you need.

We have diapers, baby food, baby formula and bottles.

If you need anything, please let me know.

P : All right. Thank you so much.

C : You're welcome, ma'am.

C : Would you like to have a bassinet for your baby?

P : Yes, I'd like to.

C : I'll set up a bassinet after take-off.

P : Thank you.

Dialogue 3

C : Excuse me. ma'am.

P1 : Yes?

C : Let me put that bag in the overhead compartment for you.
It's too big to leave under your seat.

P1 : Oh, OK. Thanks.

P2 : Excuse me. Could you please help me close this overhead compartment?
I can't get it shut.

C : Sure. Let me try.

P2 : Thank you.

Useful Expressions

*옷 입는 스타일에 관해서 말하기

You dress well.

You have a good sense of | style. / fashion.

You're | fashionable. / stylish. / overdressed. / underdressed.

You look | slender / great / sharp / elegant | in that outfit.

*성격에 관해서 묻고 답하기

What is	she he Susan	like?

What is	sort of kind of type of	a person is he?

What do you think of	her? him? my fiance?

What's your impression of	her? him? our teacher?

CHAPTER 8
PREPARATION FOR TAKE-OFF

Dialogue 1

13

C : (notice that a passenger does not have his seatbelt fastened)
Excuse me, sir. Please fasten your seatbelt now.
We will be taking off shortly. Thank you.

C : (To a child who is too small for the seatbelt)
Here, let me put this pillow under your seatbelt.
It will be more comfortable that way.

P : Thank you.

P : I don't like fastening my seatbelt.

C : I'm sorry, but I must ask you to fasten. Your seatbelt for take-off.

P : I'll just need to speak to my friend over there.

C : I understand. But, it's an Airline Regulations.

C : Excuse me.

Could you please close your tray table until after take-off? Thank you.

C : I'm sorry, sir, but you'll need to return your chair and tray table to their upright position for takeoff.

P : How do I get my chair to go back up?

I think it's stuck.

C : There's a small button on the side of the armrest. Press it and lean forward.

Dialogue 2

About restroom use

P : Excuse me. Can I use the restroom now?

C : I'm afraid not now, sir. Could you wait until after taking off, please?
We will be taking off shortly.

P : Hello. Can I go to the lavatory?

C : Yes, but please hurry up. We'll be taking off soon.

P : OK, then, I'll use the lavatory after take off.

Useful Expressions

*뭘 입고 있는지 물어보기

What are you wearing?

I'm wearing
- jeans and a red sweatshirt.
- a blue suit.
- black pants and a green sport shirt.
- a white skirt and a purple blouse.
- a pink summer dress.

What does he have on?

He has ... on.
- a brown jacket
- a yellow hat
- a red raincoat
- pink shorts and a white T-shirt

*평소에 뭘 입는지 물어보기

What do you wear to			work? school?
I	always usually sometimes	wear	a uniform to work. a suit and tie school. what's in fashion.
I	usually	dress	casually. formally.
I	like to		dress up. wear pants.

헤드폰 서비스

↓

1회용 Towel 서비스

↓

음료 서비스(Cart Service)

↓

식사 서비스(First Meal)

↓

입국서류 배포 및 작성 협조

↓

기내 판매

↓

물수건 서비스(Hot Towel)

↓

음료 서비스(Tray Base)

↓

식사 서비스(Second Meal)

↓

입국서류 작성 확인

↓

착륙 준비

장거리 비행의 서비스 순서

Dialogue 1

14

Towel Distribution

C : Would you like a hot towel, ma'am?
It's very hot. Please be careful.

Towel Pick up

C : Are you finished with your towel, ma'am?

P : Yes, I am. Thank you.

C : (Taking the towel) You're welcome.

If the passenger is sleeping

C : (Quietly and gently) Excuse me, sir.
Would you like a hot towel?

We'll be serving breakfast soon.

Headset service

C : Here's your headset ma'am.

P : No, thanks. I don't want to buy one.

C : Our headsets are free of charge.

P : In that case, I'll have it. thanks.

Movie information request

C : Here's your headset, ma'am.

P : Thank you. What movies are you showing today?

C : Today's movies are G I Joe. and Public Enemy.

P : Excuse me. When are you showing the movie?

C : About an hour later.

Dialogue 2

C : Would you carre for something to drink?

P : Yes, I'll have some juice.

P : What kind of juice do you have?

C : We have orange, pineapple, tomato and guava juice, sir.

P : I'll have orange juice.

C : Certainly, sir.

(to the next passenger)

And you, ma'am?

P : May I have a Gin & Tonic?

C : I'm sorry, ma'am.

I'm afraid we don't serve Gin on this flight.

P : Oh, I see.

I'll have some water, then.

Dialogue 3

Suggesting a cocktail

15

C : Excuse me, sir. Would you like something to drink? We have juice, cocktails, whisky and beer on this flight.

P : I want cocktails. What do you have?

C : We have Manhattan, Martini, Sloe Gin and others. Which one do you prefer?

P : Nothing in particular.

C : If you like something weak, how about a bloody mary?

P : All right. Let me try it.

C : Here you go, sir. Enjoy your drink.

Dialogue 4

Request for another round(Drink)

P : Excuse me. Could I have another drink?

C : You were drinking a Gin & Tonic, weren't you?

P : Yes, that's right.

C : Just a moment, please. Here you are.

Beverage service : Pick up

C : Excuse me, sir. Are you finished with your drink?

P : Yes, I'm finished.

C : May I take this away?

P : Sure, you will.

C : Thank you, sir.

Beverage service : Weak or strong drink

P : Excuse me. My coffee is awfully strong.

C : I'm sorry, sir. Let me change it.

P : Thank you.

Dialogue 5

16

Meal service (short portion)

C : We are now about to serve lunch, ma'am.

Would you please open your tray table?

P : What's the meal today?

C : We only have seafood today.

P : I don't like seafood.

C : I'm sorry, ma'am.

We only offer seafood on this flight.

P : Well, give me the meal anyway.

C : Here you are, ma'am.

I hope you enjoy your meal.

Dialogue 6

Meal service : on a long flight

C : Please return your seat to the upright position.

We are serving fish or beef for this flight?

P1 : Fish, please.

C : Please open your tray table.

Here you are. Take your time and enjoy your meal.

P2 : I'd like the beef, please.

C : (to T3) How about you, ma'am?

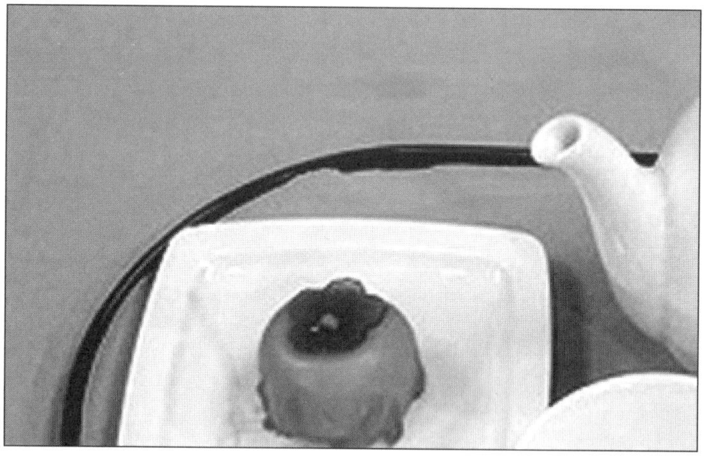

대한항공 일등석 TEA POT 기물

Dialogue 7

Meal service : Entree runs out

17

C : Excuse me, here is your meal, sir.

P : What kind of meal is this?

C : It's Korean style beef.

P : Well, I don't like beef very much. I'd like the chicken, please.

C : I'm sorry sir, but we run out of chicken today. Now we only have beef left.

P : All right. I'll take the beef then.

C : Here you are. I apologize for not being able to serve you the chicken.

We will start to serve from the back of the cabin, so, you can surely have your choice on the next serve.

P : That's great. I'll be waiting then.

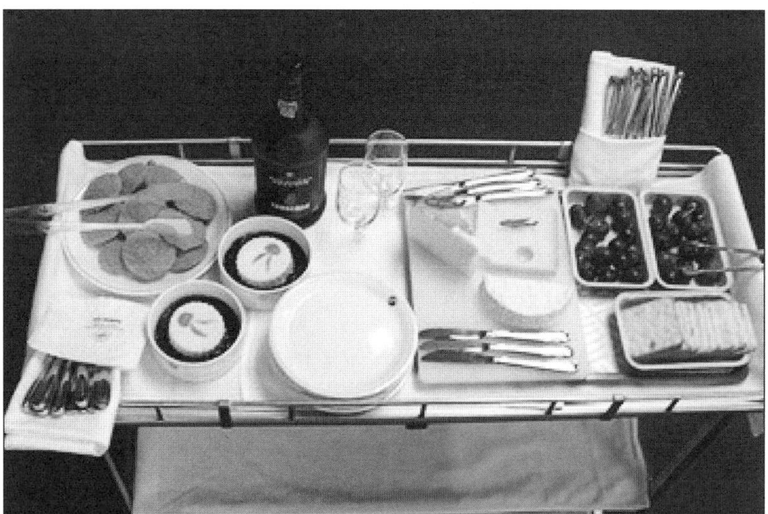

Business Class의 Cheese Presention 서비스

Dialogue 8

Special request meal

P : Miss, I requested a vegetarian meal.

C : I see. sir. I'll check it for you right away.
Just a moment, please.

(Pause)

C : Thank you for waiting.
Here you are. Enjoy your meal, sir.

C : Excuse me, sir.
Did you request a Kosher meal?

P : Yes, I did.

C : Here is your meal.

May I open your meal?

P : Yes, please.

일등석에 제공되는 샴페인(동베리뇽)과 와인

Dialogue 9

Special meal not requested

18

C : Which on would you like beef or fish, sir?

P : Are there any other choice for me? I don't like beef and I'm allergic to fish.

C : I'm sorry but, I'm afraid you Should have ordered a special meal prior to two days before the flight departure.

P : Oh, I didn't know that. I'll try to do it next time.

C : I'm sorry, sir.

Today's Tip

Special Meal

건강이나 종교, 혹은 나이, 식습관 등의 이유로 인해 항공사에서 제공하는 기내식을 섭취할 수 없는 승객들을 위한 특별식이다. 일반적으로 항공기 출발 24시간 전까지 주문 가능하다. 여러 가지 이유로 인해 일반적인 기내식의 취식이 불가한 승객들의 식사이므로, 승무원은 서비스 전 반드시 해당 승객이 주문한 식사가 맞는지를 확인해야 한다.

1) 종교로 인한 Special Meal

- Vegetarian Meal(VGML) : 채식주의자들의 식사로 주로 인도, 인도네시아인의 식사이다.
- 채식주의자라 할지라도 달걀과 우유 등이 허용되는 채식주의자와 다른 것은 완전히 배제하는 엄격한 채식주의자로 나누어진다.
- Kosher Meal(KSML) : 유대 정교자들의 율법에 의해 조리된 식사로 돼지고기는 사용하지 않으며 다른 육류도 기도를 올린 것에 한하여 사용된다. KSML은 반드시 해당 승객에게 개봉 의사 여부를 확인한 후에 Heating할 수 있다.
- Hindu Meal(HNML) : 쇠고기를 먹지 않는 힌두교도들을 위한 식사이다.
- Moslem Meal(MOML) : 돼지고기를 취식하지 않는 이슬람교도들을 위한 기내식이다.

2) 건강으로 인한 Special Meal

- No dairy Products : 식사의 재료에 우유가 들어가지 않는 것으로 우유분해 효소가 없는 승객의 식사이다.
- DBMl(Diabetic Meal) : 당뇨환자용 식사이다.

Today's Tip

- GFML(Gluten Free) : 글루텐이 들어가지 않은 것으로 내장질환 소아용 식사이다.
- LFML(Low Fat) : 저콜레스테롤 저지방 식사로 심장질환 동맥경화 등의 성인질환 승객의 식사이다.
- SBML(Soft Blend Diet Meal) : 위염이나 위궤양 환자에게 제공되는 무자극성 기내식이다.

3) 어린이를 위한 Special Meal

- IFML(Infant Meal), BBML(baby Meal) : 유아들의 식사로 주로 이유와 이유식이 제공된다.
- TDML(Toddler Meal) : 2세에서 6세 정도의 어린이를 위한 기내식이다. 씹기 쉬운 형태로 조리된다.
- CHML(Child Meal) : 12세까지 어린이의 기내식으로 햄버거, 피자, 스파게티, 샌드위치, 김밥 등이 있으며 어린이들이 좋아하는 초콜릿과 음료가 함께 준비되어 플라스틱 박스째로 제공된다.

4) 기타 Special Meal

- SPMA(Anniversary Cake) : 결혼이나 축하 기념 케이크가 있으며, 승무원은 샴페인과 함께 축하의 메시지와 케이크를 서비스한다.
- SFML(Seafood Meal) : 해산물로 구성된 기내식이다.

Today's Tip

기내음료

일반적으로 음료라 하는 것은 알코올을 함유한 음료와 비알코올 음료를 모두 포함하는 말이다. 인간의 신체 구성요소 중 70% 이상이 수분으로 구성되어 있음을 감안할 때, 건조한 기내에서 건강한 여행을 즐기기 위해서는 적절한 수분 섭취가 필요하며, 승무원은 충분한 음료 서비스를 실시해야 한다.

1) 비알코올 음료

- Juice류 : Orange, Apple, pine apple, tomato Juice, Guava
- Coffee류 : Decaffeinated Coffee, Instant Coffee, Roasted Coffee
- Tea류 : Black Tea, Green tea, 우롱차, 인삼차
- 탄산음료 : Coke, Sprite, Soda Water, Tonic, Gingerale

2) 알코올 음료

- Wine과 Sparkling, Wine, liqueur, Beer, Gin, Vodka

Dialogue 10

Drink service during the meal

C : Would you care for some coffee or tea?

P : No thanks. Could I have another beer, instead?

C : Certainly. Here you are. Enjoy your meal.

(To next passenger) What about you ma'am?

Would you like some more wine?

P2 : Yes, please. That would be great.

C : Here you are.

C : Coffee or tea, ma'am?

P : I'll have some tea please.

And could I have some milk for my son.

C : Certainly, ma'am. May I have your cup, please?

Thank you. Here's your tea and milk.

P : Thank you very much.

C : My pleasure ma'am. Enjoy your meal.

Dialogue 11

19

Wine service

C : Would you like some wine to go with your salmon?

P : Yes, please.

C : Which would you prefer, red or white wine?

P : White, please.

C : Here you are.

P : Thank you.

Wine Service : refill

P : Can I have some more wine?

C : Did you have white wine?

P : Yes, I did. Thank you.

Useful Expressions

*좋은 성격에 관해서 말하기

She is / He		
	active.	
	easy to get along with.	
	friendly.	
	fun.	

She is / He		
	a generous	person.
	kind	
	an intelligent	
	honest	

She seems like a / He		
	patient	person.
	reserved	
	talented	
	warm	

*나쁜 성격에 관해서 말하기

She is He	arrogant. boring. careless. difficult to approach.

She is He	a an	hot-tempered loud impatient inconsiderate	person.

She seems like a He	bossy picky sensitive rude	person.

*성격의 장점과 약점에 관해서 말하기

What are your strengths?

I make friends easily.
I'm optimistic about everything.
My friends say I'm always cheerful.
I can cooperate with anybody.
I think I'm both sensitive and brave.

What are your weaknesses?

I'm not really sociable.
I'm sort of a pessimist.
I tend to be withdrawn.
I'm unable to make decisions.
I sometimes speak too much.

Dialogue 12

Meal tray pick-up

C : Excuse me, sir.

Are you done with your meal?

P : Yes, I am.

C : May I take your meal tray?

P : Of course.

C : Did you enjoy your meal. sir?

P : Yes, It was delicious.

C : Are you finished with your meal?

P : No, I'm not finished yet.

C : I'm sorry, ma'am.

Please take your time and enjoy your meal.

P : Thank you.

C : Would you like some more coffee or tea?

P : I want some coffee, please.

C : I'll get some for you right away.

Just a moment, please.

Here you are.

Dialogue 13

20

In–flight sales : Shopping guide

C : Would you like to buy any duty-free items?

P : What kind of items do you have?

C : Here is the shopping guide. sir.

C : Would you like to buy something, sir?

P : Yes, what do you have?

C : Here is the shopping guide. It will help you with the items we have.

P : Thank you.

Dialogue 14

In-flight sales : (General)

C : Would you like to buy something?

P : Could I have two cartons of Dunhill and a bottle of Chivas Regal, please.

C : Certainly. Here you are. That will be $150, please.

P : Here you are.

C : Would you like to buy something from the duty free?

P : Could I have two cartons of Kent and a bottle of Ballentine's 17 years old, please.

C : Certainly. here you are. That will be $170, please.

P : Do you accept cards?

C : Yes, We do.

C : Here's your change, ma'am.

P : Keep the change.

C : Thank you. But we are not allowed to accept tips.

Dialogue 15

21

Sold Out

C : Would you like to buy any duty free items?

P : Yes, I'd like a bottle of old parr, please.

C : I'm sorry, but it's sold out.

Would you like another items instead?

Dialogue 16

In-flight sales : Change not available

P : Excuse me. All I have is a 100 dollar bill. Do you have any change?

C : I'm sorry, sir. I'm afraid I don't have change right now, but I'll bring your change soon.

(Pause)

Thank you for waiting.

Here is your change, sir.

P : Thank you.

Dialogue 17

Acceptable currency

C : Here you are. That will be 40 dollars, sir.

P : I don't have any dollars. Do you accept thailand baht?

C : I'm sorry, sir. I am afraid we do not accept Thailand Baht. Do you have any other currency?

P : I have some Korean won.

C : That'll be fine, sir.

Dialogue 18

Document Service : Entering Korea

22

P : Miss. I'm a tourist.

C : Yes, sir.

All foreigners entering Korea must fill out the ED card and the Customs form.

P : I see.

Do you have an English form for customs?

C : Yes, sir.

Here you are, sir.

Dialogue 19

Entering the U.S.A.

P : Do I need these cards?

C : Are you a U.S. citizen or a resident?

P : Yes, I'm a U.S. citizen.

C : Then you only need customs form.

C : Are you a U.S. citizen or a resident?

P : No, I'm german.

C : Then you'll need the entry card and the customs form.

P : Do I need these cards?

I live in the U.S., but I'm not a citizen yet.

C : Do you have an alien registration card?

P : Yes, I do.

C : Then you only need the customs declaration form, sir.

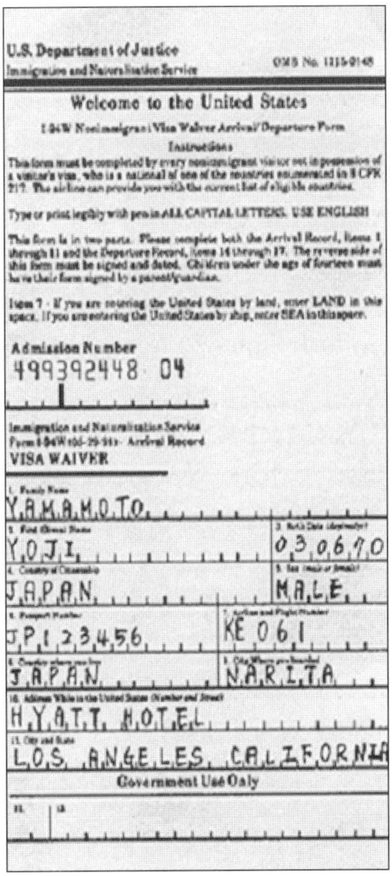

U.S. Department of Justice
Immigration and Naturalization Service
OMB No. 1115-0148

Welcome to the United States

I-94W Nonimmigrant Visa Waiver Arrival/Departure Form

Instructions

This form must be completed by every nonimmigrant visitor not in possession of a visitor's visa, who is a national of one of the countries enumerated in 8 CFR 217. The airline can provide you with the current list of eligible countries.

Type or print legibly with pen in ALL CAPITAL LETTERS. USE ENGLISH

This form is in two parts. Please complete both the Arrival Record, Items 1 through 11 and the Departure Record, Items 14 through 17. The reverse side of this form must be signed and dated. Children under the age of fourteen must have their form signed by a parent/guardian.

Item 7 - If you are entering the United States by land, enter LAND in this space. If you are entering the United States by ship, enter SEA in this space.

Admission Number
499392448 04

Immigration and Naturalization Service
Form I-94W - Arrival Record
VISA WAIVER

1. Family Name: YAMAMOTO
2. First (Given) Name: YOJI
3. Birth Date: 03 06 70
4. Country of Citizenship: JAPAN
5. Sex (male or female): MALE
6. Passport Number: JP123456
7. Airline and Flight Number: KE 061
8. Country where you live: JAPAN
9. City Where you boarded: NARITA
10. Address While in the United States (Number and Street): HYATT HOTEL
11. City and State: LOS ANGELES, CALIFORNIA

Government Use Only

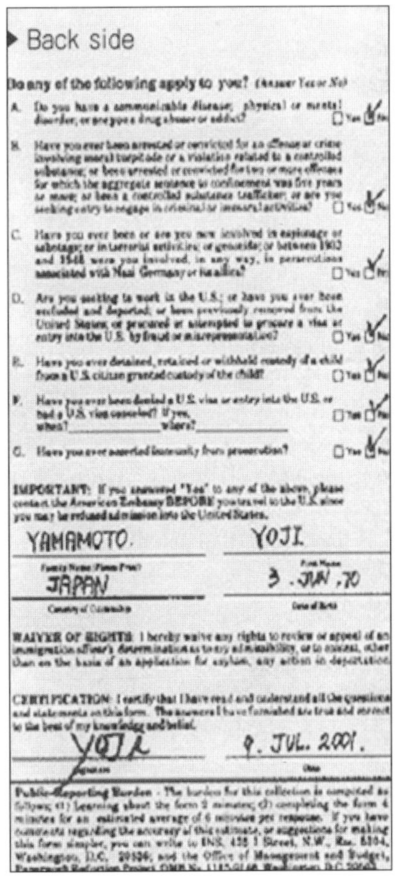

▶ Back side

Do any of the following apply to you? (Answer Yes or No)

A. Do you have a communicable disease; physical or mental disorder; or are you a drug abuser or addict? ☐ Yes ☑ No

B. Have you ever been arrested or convicted for an offense or crime involving moral turpitude or a violation related to a controlled substance; or been arrested or convicted for two or more offenses for which the aggregate sentence to confinement was five years or more; or been a controlled substance trafficker; or are you seeking entry to engage in criminal or immoral activities? ☐ Yes ☑ No

C. Have you ever been or are you now involved in espionage or sabotage; or in terrorist activities; or genocide; or between 1933 and 1945 were you involved, in any way, in persecutions associated with Nazi Germany or its allies? ☐ Yes ☑ No

D. Are you seeking to work in the U.S.; or have you ever been excluded and deported; or been previously removed from the United States; or procured or attempted to procure a visa or entry into the U.S. by fraud or misrepresentation? ☐ Yes ☑ No

E. Have you ever detained, retained or withheld custody of a child from a U.S. citizen granted custody of the child? ☐ Yes ☑ No

F. Have you ever been denied a U.S. visa or entry into the U.S. or had a U.S. visa canceled? If yes, when? ______ where? ______ ☐ Yes ☑ No

G. Have you ever asserted immunity from prosecution? ☐ Yes ☑ No

IMPORTANT: If you answered "Yes" to any of the above, please contact the American Embassy BEFORE you travel to the U.S. since you may be refused admission into the United States.

YAMAMOTO. — Family Name (Please Print)
YOJI — First Name
JAPAN — Country of Citizenship
3. JUN. 70 — Date of Birth

WAIVER OF RIGHTS: I hereby waive any rights to review or appeal of an immigration officer's determination as to my admissibility, or to contest, other than on the basis of an application for asylum, any action in deportation.

CERTIFICATION: I certify that I have read and understand all the questions and statements on this form. The answers I have furnished are true and correct to the best of my knowledge and belief.

YOJI — Signature
9. JUL. 2001. — Date

Public Reporting Burden - The burden for this collection is computed as follows: (1) Learning about the form 2 minutes; (2) completing the form 4 minutes for an estimated average of 6 minutes per response. If you have comments regarding the accuracy of this estimate, or suggestions for making this form simpler, you can write to INS, 425 I Street, N.W., Rm. 5304, Washington, D.C. 20536; and the Office of Management and Budget, Paperwork Reduction Project, OMB No. 1115-0148, Washington, D.C. 20503.

미국 입국 서류

Dialogue 20

23 C : Excuse me, sir. Are you an American citizen?

P : No, I'm not.

C : Do you have a visa for the United States?

P : Yes, I do.

C : Could you fill out this entry card before we arrive, please? It's for immigration.

P : All right.

C : Thank you.

P : Oh, I forgot to bring something to write with. Do you have a pen?

C : Here you are.

Dialogue 21

Questions from Passengers : Flight time

P : How long will it take to Los Angeles?

C : Our scheduled flight time will be 9 hours and 20 minutes today.

P : What's the time difference between Seoul & Los Angeles?

C : Seoul is 16 hours ahead of Los Angeles.

P : I see. thank you.

C : You're welcome, sir.

Dialogue 22

Arrival Time

C : Would you like some coffee, sir?

P : Yes, that will be great.

By the way, how long will it take to Honolulu?

C : We will arrive in about 3 hours from now.

P : I see. Thank you.

Useful Expressions

*어떤 사람을 알고 있는지에 관해서 묻고 답하기

Who is	he? she?	
Do you know	who he is? what he does? where he's from? anything about him?	
Do you know	him her	well?
I know	of somewhat about nothing about	him. her.

*습관에 관해서 묻고 답하기

Do you have a habit?

I have a habit of
- licking my lips when I'm nervous.
- taking a walk when it rains.
- drinking coffee after every meal.

I'm in the habit of
- talking too much when i'm nervous.
- eating when I'm stressed out.
- looking in the mirror every five minutes.

I'm not in the habit of
- lying.
- borrowing money.
- go shopping everyday.

I broke the habit of
- smoking in the morning.
- oversleeping.
- being late to school.

*관심 분야에 관해서 묻고 답하기

What are your interests?

I'm into	dancing swimming drinking	these days. now
I am not into	modern music romantic novels computer games	any more.

I have little interest in those things.

Dialogue 23

No Time difference

24

P : May I ask a question?

C : Yes, you may.

P : What's the time difference between Seoul and Narita?

C : There is no time difference between these two cities.

Time difference

P : How much is the time difference between Seoul and New York?

C : There is a 14 hour difference between Seoul and New York. New York is 14 hours behind Seoul.

Dialogue 24

Turbulence

C : Could you fasten your seatbelt, sir?

P : Excuse me?

C : The pilots turned on the fasten seatbelt sign.
We may be having some turbulence.

P : Oh, really? Nothing serious, I hope.

C : I hope not. Oops.

P : Excuse me. Could I have a safety instruction card?
I can't find one in the seat pocket.

C : Let me get you one.

P : Can I use the lavatory?

C : Sorry. You aren't allowed to leave your seat right now.

Dialogue 25

25 C : Ma'am, you're free to get up and walk around the cabin, now.

The fasten seatbelt sign has been turned off.

P1 : Good. Thank you.

P2 : Excuse me. It's very chilly in here. Do you have an extra blanket?

C : Yes, I'll bring you a blanket.

P2 : By the way. What's our ETA?

C : We were due in at 5:00 p.m., but I think we're going to be late.

P1 : Will you show me a brochure for duty-free items?

C : Yes. I'll back in a minute.

Dialogue 26

Sick Passenger

(Pax call chimes)

C : Yes, ma'am, May I help you?

P : Yes, I have a terrible headache.

Do you have some medicine?

C : I'm sorry, to hear that, ma'am.

We have Tylenol on board.

Are you allergic to any medicine?

P : No. I am not.

C : I see, I'll get some for you right away.

(pause)

C : Here you are. I hope you will feel better soon.

P : Thank you.

Dialogue 27

26

Medicine for airsick

P : Excuse me, miss. I get airsick very easily.

I feel dizzy.

Do you have anything for that?

C : I'm sorry to hear that, sir. We have bonamin.

Would that be alright?

P : Yes, that's alright.

C : Just a moment, please.

(pause)

C : I hope you feel better.

Dialogue 28

Medicine for indigestion

P : Excuse me, miss. Do you have anything for indigestion?

C : Yes, sir. We have Festal on board.
Are you allergic to any medication?

P : No, I am not.

C : I'll get one for you ASAP.

(Pause)

C : Here you are. I hope you get well soon.

Dialogue 29

NO SMOKING

C : Excuse me, sir.

Smoking is not allowed during the entire flight.

P : Oh, I am sorry.

C : Thank you.

Useful Expressions

*취미에 관해서 묻고 답하기

What is your hobby?

Do you have any particular hobbies?

What do you do for recreation? / fun?

What do you do in your spare / free time?

How do you like to spend / spare your free time?

I	read. exercise. collect stamps. go to the movies. go to art galleries. listen to music.

＊좋아하는 타입의 이성에 관해서 묻고 답하기

What is your hobby?

Are you	seeing dating	anyone?

Do you have a	girlfriend? boyfriend?

What's your type?

What	type / kind	of	a man / a woman / a person	do you like? / do you want to marry?

I like	a man / a woman / someone	who is	tall and handsome. / very feminine. / generous and flexible. / romantic and ambitious.

I like	a man / a woman / someone	with	a sense of humor. / long hair. / good education.

*감정에 관한 표현(About Feelings)

happy

I'm excited.	I'm pleased.
I'm so delighted.	I'm so glad.
I'm very happy.	I am as happy as I can be.

Sad

I'm depressed. I'm feeling blue.
I'm not myself. I'm so sad.
I'm not in a good mood right now.
I feel miserable.
I've been feeling down lately. I feel gloomy.

Angry

I'm mad at him.	I'm a little annoyed.
I lost my temper.	I'm so pissed off.
I'm irritated.	I'm so pissed off.
I'm upset.	I'm furious.
I've had it.	I can't stand it any more.

Scared

I'm afraid.	I'm frightened.
I'm scared.	I'm terrified.
I'm scared to death.	I have a fear of heights.

Bored

I'm bored.	I'm bored to death.
I'm bored out of my mind.	It puts me to sleep.

Surprised

I'm amazed.	I'm shocked.
What a surprise!	You surprised me.

Sympathy

How awful!	How terrible!
I feel sorry for her.	What a pity!
I want to express my sympathy.	You poor thing.

Disappointed

I'm disappointed.	I'm disappointed in you.
I won't let it get to me.	You really let me do down.

Relieved

I'm so relieved.	What a relief!
It puts my mind at ease.	That's a load off my mind.

Indifference

I don't care.	Suit yourself.
It has nothing to do with me.	Who cares?

Embarrassed

I'm so embarrassed.	I feel ashamed.

Dialogue 1

27 P : Excuse me, Miss. May I have some coffee, please?

C : I'm sorry, sir. We've closed for landing.

P : No, I don't mind at all.

C : Thank you. sir.

Dialogue 2

C : Excuse me, sir. We'll be landing at Inchon international airport shortly.

Can I have your earphone set, please?

P : Here is it. Would you take this used cup?

C : Thank you.

P : You're welcome.

Dialogue 3

C : Could you put your seat forward now, ma'am?
We'll be landing shortly.

P : So soon? great.

C : And I'm also collecting the headsets. Would you mind passing them to me, please?

P : No problem. Here you go.

Dialogue 4

28 C : Excuse me, sir.

Did you fasten your seatbelt? We'll be landing shortly.

Thank you.

C : Would you please return your seat upright for landing?

P : I see.

C : Would you mind closing your tray table, too?

We'll be landing soon.

C : Excuse me, ma'am.

Would you please keep your bag under the seat until after landing?

It might fall out during landing.

P : O.K.

Dialogue 5

Returning passenger's personal belongings

P : Would you bring me the bag I gave you earlier?

C : Yes, sir. I'll be right back.

(pause)

Here you are.

P : Thank you.

C : You're welcome, sir.

I hope to see you on board again soon.

Useful Expressions

*Describing appearances

1. A : What does your sister look like?

   B : Well, she has straight blond hair and blue eyes.

   A : Is she tall or short?

   B : She's fairly tall.

   A : Is she fat or thin?

   B : Let's see. She's thin.

2. A : You look different today.

   B : I've changed my hair style.

   A : I love that hair style. It looks good on you.

   B : Thank you!

3. A : How tall are you?

   B : I'm 5 feet 7 inches tall.

4. A : Does he wear glasses?

   B : Yes, he does.

   A : Does he have a mustache?

   B : No, he doesn't.

5. A : Who is Jim?

   B : Jim is the tall guy. He's wearing glasses.

6. A : Susan, what color are your eyes?

   B : They're brown. Why?

   A : They look blue today.

   B : Oh, I'm wearing colored contact lens.

7. A : Excuse me. Have you seen my daughter?

   B : What does she look like?

   A : She's about three feet tall with curly red hair.

Dialogue 1

29

During taxiing

P : (Standing and getting bags from overhead during taxiing)

C : Excuse me. Would you please remain seated until the plane completely stops?

It's for your safety.

P : Oh, I'm sorry.

Dialogue 2

Saying good-bye : farewell

C : Good-bye, sir. Thank you for flying with Asiana Airlines. We hope to see you on board again.

P : Good-bye. I enjoyed flight.

C : Have a good trip in Seoul.

Useful Expressions

*Describing personalities

1. A : Do you know John?
   B : Yes, he's in my history class.
   A : What's he like?
   B : He's nice and very clever.

2. A : Have you heard anything about the new student in our class?
   B : Yes. People say she's very nice.
   A : What else have you heard?
   B : Well, they also say she's very outgoing.

3. A : You seem to be a shy person.
   B : Sort of. But once I get to know someone, I can be funny and outgoing.
   A : Really? Then, Maybe I should get to know you better.

4. A : I've heard that Peter is mean and selfish.

   B : You'd better stay away from him.

5. A : I can't get along with Nick.

   B : Why not?

   A : He's too lazy. He always leaves the dishes in the sink.

   B : You should try to talk to him.

6. A : I wonder if Sam will change after we get married.

   B : Dream on. You can't change someone's personality.

   A : Why not?

   B : Because he was born like that.

7. A : What do you think of Min-Hee?

   B : I like her, But she talks too much!

   A : Oh, really?

   B : I sometimes have a headache when I listen to her talking.

PART 2

TOURISM ENGLISH

Dialogue 1

CHAPTER 1
HOTEL RESERVATION

30

A : Tour Counselor, B : Guest

A : Good afternoon. Lucy Travel Agency, may I help you?

B : Yes. I'm planning a business trip to LA for 6 days from June 4th. Can you recommend a good hotel downtown?

A : Yes. We have several deluxe hotels located in downtown.

B : How can I get to the hotel from the airport? This is my first visit to LA and I have lots of baggages.

A : Don't worry, sir. If you want, the hotel will arrange limousine service to pick you up.

B : How far is the hotel from the airport?

A : It depends on traffic congestion in the city, but usually it'll take about 1 hour by car.

B : Please fix me up with a room at the Star hotel for 6 nights from June 4th and also arrange pick up service for me at the airport.

A : O.K. We'll prepare a room and transportation for you when you arrive in LA. And would you fill up this travel request form, please?

B : Sure... Here you go.

Dialogue 2

A : Desk Clerk, B : Caller

A : Seoul Hotel. How may I help you?

B : Yes. Do you have any rooms available for tomorrow?

A : Let's see.
We have some rooms available tomorrow.
Would you like a single or a double?

B : Are there any deluxe suites available?

A : I'm sorry, all deluxe suites are fully booked.
How would you like a double room with a fine view?

B : What's the room like?

A : It's on the 3rd floor commanding a fine view of Mt. Namsan.
It's also a very quiet room.

B : That sounds good.

Dialogue 3

31

A : Desk Clerk, B : Guest, C : Reservation Clerk

A : Hello, Pacific Hotel. Can I help you?

B : Yes, I need to make a room reservation.

A : Hold on, please. I'll connect you with our reservation department.

C : Reservation office, how may I help you?

B : Can I book a room in your hotel for 5 nights from May 10th?

C : Just a moment, sir. I'll check if there is any room available. I'm sorry, sir. All rooms are occupied except suit rooms. Would that be all right, sir?

B : What's a suite?

C : It's a more spacious room. It comes with separate living room and bed room.

B : Sounds great. But it must be very expensive.

C : Compared to regular rooms the difference is $100 for one day. Would you like me to book for you?

B : Oh, that's too expensive.

C : Then we can put you on the waiting list. Would that be alright?

B : That will be better.

Dialogue 4

A : Reservation Clerk, B : Jeeny Lee

A : Good afternoon. Reservation desk. Kim Speaking.

B : Yes, I'd like to make a reservation.

A : What kind of room would you like?

B : A double with bath.

A : How long would you like to stay?

B : From August 1st to August 30th.

A : Would you like a room with an ocean view or a mountain view?

B : With a mountain view, please.

A : We have a room with a nice mountain view of Mt. Namsan.

B : That's very good. I'll take it.

A : May I have your name, please?

B : Yes, Jeeny Lee.

A : I'm looking forward to seeing you on August 1st.

B : Thank you. Good Bye.

Dialogue 5

A : Reservation Clerk, B : Jeeny Lee

A : Good morning. Room reservation. Lee speaking. Can I help you?

B : Yes, I'd like to know if I can change my reservation date or not.

A : May I have your name and your expected arrival date, please?

B : My name is Jeeny Lee.
I am supposed to be there on July 20th but I'd like to delay the arrival date to August 4th. Would that be possible?

A : Just a moment.
I'm afraid but we're fully booked on that date.

B : Well, is there any way I could get a room?

A : We can put you on the waiting list or arrange you at another hotel around here.

B : Please put me on the waiting list.

A : Very well.

CHAPTER 2
CHECK-IN

Dialogue 1

32

A : Bellman, B : Customer

A : Welcome to Namsan Hotel. May I help you with your baggage?

B : Yes, please.

A : Do you have any baggage in the trunk?

B : Yes, I have 2 more bags in the trunk.

A : O.K., ma'am. I'll make sure you have everything.
Please go inside, I'll bring in your bags.

B : Thank you.

A : You're welcome.

Dialogue 2

A : Bellman, B : Guest

A : Good afternoon. May I help you, sir?

B : Yes, please. I have two baggages in my car trunk.
Would you bring those baggages to room 556 for me?

A : Yes, sir. Let me carry your baggages to room 556.

B : Thanks a lot.

A : Please watch out of the revolving door. The inside door is automatic.

B : Thank you for saying that. By the way, where can I register?

A : You can register at the front desk right over there.

Dialogue 3

33 *A : Receptionist, B : Jeeny Lee*

A : May I help you, Miss?

B : Yes. I have a reservation.

A : May I have your name?

B : My name is Jeeny Lee.

A : That's strange. Your name doesn't seem to be here.

B : It could be under my father's name, Peter Lee.

A : Yes, we have your reservation under the name of Peter Lee. Would you like to fill out this registration form?

B : OK... Here you are.

A : Thank you. And you'll be in room 855 – that's on the third floor.

B : Thanks for helping.

A : My pleasure.

Dialogue 4

A : Receptionist, B : Bill

A : How may I help you?

B : We don't have a reservation.
Do you have two single rooms available for tonight?

A : I'm sorry, but those rooms are booked up already.
But we have some double rooms left.

B : Are those rooms next to each other?

A : Yes. There are.

B : That's great.

A : Would you like to sign this registration form, please?

B : Sure.

A : You will be in room 712 and room 713.
Bellman will bring up your luggages.
Enjoy your stay.

B : Thank you.

Dialogue 5

34

A : Receptionist, B : Mr. and Mrs. Kim

A : Good afternoon. May I help you?

B : Do you have a room in the name of Mr. and Mrs. Kim?

A : Let me check. Yes, we do have a reservation for you.

B : I booked a double room but don't you have a twin room available?

A : Yes, we do. It has a nice view of Waikiki beach.

B : Well, does the bathroom have a tub?

A : Yes, it does have a large tub.

B : That's good. I think that will do.

A : How long do you want to stay?

B : For 4 days, until the 10th.

A : Alright. Please sign here.

Dialogue 6

A : Receptionist, B : Jason Kim

A : Welcome to the Pacific Hotel, sir!
Do you have a reservation with us?
B : Yes, we do. My name is Jason Kim.
A : Just one moment, sir... You are Mr. Kim.
B : Yes, that's right.
A : You reserved a double room for three nights, didn't you?
B : Yes, I did.
A : Your room is ready, sir. It's number 656, which has a fine ocean view. Please fill out this registration form and I'll get your key.
B : OK... Here's the form. Are your restaurants still open?
A : Yes, sir, they are open until 10 p.m. and the coffee shop until 2 a.m.
B : How about the exercise facilities?
A : You can use the fitness club and pool anytime you like.
B : That's good.
A : Do you have any valuables that you would like for us to keep in our hotel safe?
B : I guess we don't.
A : Here is your key, and this bellman will carry your bags to your room.
B : Thanks a lot.
A : Enjoy your stay.

Dialogue 1

35

A : Room Service, B : Guest

A : Good morning, Room service. May I help you?

B : Hello, Are you finished serving breakfast?

A : No, sir. Breakfast menu is until 10:00 a.m.

B : Good. Then, can I have a continental breakfast?

A : You have a choice of cereal or fruit juice, sir?

B : Fruit juice, please.

A : And tea or coffee?

B : Coffee please. Also, I want to order two sunny sides up with french fries.

A : Anything else?

B : No, thank you.

Dialogue 2

A : Room Service, B : Peter Park

A : Room service, may I help you?

B : Yes. I'd like to have American breakfast in my room tomorrow morning.

A : Which do you like orange juice or tomato juice?

B : Orange juice would be better.

A : How would you like your eggs?

B : Sunny-side up, please.

A : All right, sir. Which would you like coffee or tea?

B : Black tea, please.

A : May I have your room number?

B : My name is Peter Park in room 507.

A : What time would you like it served, sir?

B : At 7:30 a.m.
Be sure they aren't too cold.

A : I'll leave a note for you.

B : Thank you.

Dialogue 3

36

A : Room Service, B : Guest

A : (knocking on the door) Hello. Room service.

B : Come on in.

A : I've brought your lunch you ordered, sir. Where do you want me to put it?

B : Over there by the window will be fine.

A : Shall I pour you a cup of coffee straightaway?

B : No thanks! I'll take care of it.

A : Is there anything else you need?

B : No, I don't think so. Everything is just perfect.

A : Enjoy your lunch.

Dialogue 4

A : Waiter, B : Guest

A : Good morning, sir. May I take your order now?

B : Yes, I'll have American breakfast.

A : What kind of juice do you want? We have orange, grapefruit, and tomato juice.

B : I'll have a tomato juice.

A : OK, and you also get two eggs cooked as you wish.

B : Boiled, please. And I'll have cereals, please.

A : Yes, sir. Coffee or tea?

B : A cup of tea please, with sugar and lemon.

A : All right. I'll bring them right away, sir.

Dialogue 5

A : Waiter, B : Guest

A : Are you ready to order now?

B : Could we have a few minutes, please?

A : No problem, Take your time.

(pause)

A : Have you decided yet?

B : Yes. I'll have the grilled chicken breast.

A : How about bread?

B : What kind of bread do you have?

A : We have hard and soft rolls.

B : Soft rolls, please.

A : What kind of dressing would you like?

B : Oil and vinegar on thc side, please.

A : Would you like some sauce for your chicken?

B : Yes, please.

A : I'll have your grilled chicken breast in a minute.

B : Thank you.

Dialogue 6

37

A : Waiter, B : Guest

A : Good evening, ma'am. Here is your menu.

B : Everything looks good.

A : What would you like this evening?

B : I'd like a steak, please.

A : How would you like your steak?

B : Medium, please. And can I have it with rice instead of potato?

A : And what kind of soup would you like to have?

B : Well. What's the soup of the day?

A : Today we have vegetable soup. it's made of tomatoes and fresh vegetable.

B : I'll take that.

A : Would you like to drink?

B : Cold water with ice would be fine.

A : So, that's a medium steak with rice and a vegetable soup.

B : Alright, thank you.

Dialogue 7

A : Waiter, B : Guest

B : What do you recommend for us, today?

A : Our daily special is New York Sirloin steak.
I am sure you will like it, sir.

B : Sounds good. We will have that.

A : How would you like your steak

B : Well done, please. How about you Daniel?

C : Medium rare, please.

A : How would you like your potatoes?

B : I want mashed potatoes.

C : I'll have french fires.

A : Would you like to order dessert now?

B : No, after meal, please.

A : Thank you.

Dialogue 8

38 *A : Launderer, B : Guest*

A : Laundry service.

I have brought your laundry, sir.

B : Come on in.

A : Please check it if it is correct.

B : Should I pay in cash?

A : As you like, sir.

You can pay in cash or sign for it so that you can pay later when you check out, sir.

B : Then, I'd like to sign for it.

A : No problem.

Dialogue 9

Locations and Directions

① **A** : Which room is Mr. In?
B : Let me check. Yes, he's in room 707.
A : Where can I find room 707?
B : Take the elevator on your left. turn right when you come out of the elevator.

② **C** : Excuse me, where's the coffee shop?
D : It's on this floor. Just across the lobby, You'll see it at the end of the corridor.

③ **E** : Can I buy stamps in the hotel?
F : Yes, Ma'am, at the gift shop on the 2nd floor.

④ **G** : I have a meeting at the conference room. Could you tell me where it is?
H : Yes, sir. It's on the 2nd floor. Take the escalator the turn left and the conference suite is just on your right.

Dialogue 1

39

A : Housekeeping, B : John Kim

A : Hello, this is housekeeping. May I help you?

B : Yes. This is John Kim in room 704.
The room is too hot.
I think the air conditioner is out of order.
Could you send someone to fix it up right away?

A : I'm sorry for the inconvenience. Let me check for you. There is temperature control panel on the wall. Is it properly adjusted?

B : Sure, but thermostat doesn't seem to work.
I couldn't sleep well.

A : I'll send an engineer to take care of it right away.
Is there anything else?

B : No, that's all. Thank you.

Dialogue 2

A : Guest, B : Operator

A : Operator, did anyone call me up while I was out?

B : Yes, there was a phone call from Mr. Park.

A : What did he say?

B : He said you call him up when you arrived.

A : Oh, I see. Thanks a lot. And I'll be out for 2 hours again. I expect another call after that. If you receive the call could you please tell the person to come to the hotel?

B : Yes. I will.

A : OK. thank you.

Dialogue 3

40

A : Operator, B : Heesoo Kim, C : Front Deck Clerk

A : Good evening, operator.

B : This is Heesoo Kim in room 605.
I'd like to have a wake-up call at 6 o'clock in the morning.

A : Hold on please. I'll connect you to the front desk.

C : Front desk. How may I help you?

B : Can you give me a wake-up call at 6:00 o'clock in the morning?

C : May I have your name and room number.

B : My name is Heesoo Kim in room 605.

C : Yes, Ms. Kim in room 605, wake-up call at 6 o'clock in the morning.
I'll take care of it by myself.

Dialogue 4

A : Meejin Lee, B : Operator

A : Operator? This is Meejin Lee in room 806.
I'd like to make an overseas call to Seoul.

B : Is it a person-to-person call?

A : Yes. The party I want to call is Choelsu Lee.

B : What number do you wish to call?

A : Area code 01 and the number is 342-1456.

B : Very well, Ms. Lee. I'll call you back as soon as your party is on the line.
(pause)

A : Hello, Meejin Lee speaking.

B : Hello, this is operator. Your party is on the line. Go ahead.

A : Thanks.

Dialogue 5

41

A : Front Desk Clerk, B : Guest

A : Good evening, this is Pacific hotel. May I help you?

B : Could you tell me if Mrs. William is staying in the hotel?

A : Hold on, please. I'll check to see. I'm sorry. There is no one here by that name in any other room. Maybe you have the wrong hotel.

B : I'm sorry but, can you check again?

A : How do you spell his name?

B : That's W-I-L-L-I-A-M.

Dialogue 6

A : Clerk, B : Linda Kim

A : Swiss Hotel. May I help you?

B : This is Linda Kim calling from Korea.
Can I speak to Mr. Brown in room 545.

A : Just a moment... Hello? I'm sorry, Mr. Brown just stepped out of his room.

B : What time do you expect him back?

A : He won't be back until 7 p.m.
When he returns to the hotel, shall I have him call you back?

B : That would be nice. Just tell him that Ms. Kim called.
He's got my number.

A : Very well, Ms. Kim. I'll give Mr. Brown the message.

Dialogue 1

CHAPTER 5
CHECK-OUT

42

A : Guest, B : Clerk

A : I'm checking out. Can you prepare my bill, please?

B : It's all prepared for you, sir.

A : Oh, good, then I'll settle it now.

B : How are you paying, sir?

A : I'd like to pay with Visa card. Is it Okay?

B : Certainly, sir. Here is your bill.

A : Everything looks in order. Is service charge and tax included?

B : Yes, they are all included in your bill. Would you please sign here on the bottom?

A : Oh, sure.

B : Thank you, Here is your receipt and your credit card. I hope you enjoyed your stay with us.

A : If I visit here again, I'll choose your hotel again.

B : Thank you so much, sir.

Dialogue 2

A : Guest, B : Clerk

A : I'm going to check out today.
What is the check-out time?

B : 11 a.m., sir.

A : Do you charge for another day if I do not vacate my room by 11 a.m.?

B : Yes, we do.

A : I didn't know that.
I'm going to leave my room by 11 a.m.

B : Could you tell me your room number?

A : Yes, room 545.

B : You stayed for three nights, didn't you?

A : Yes, I did.
How much does the bill come to?

B : It comes to a total of $520.
How would you like to pay?

A : Do you accept traveler's check?

B : Certainly, sir.

Dialogue 3

43

A : Clerk, B : Jeeny Lee

A : Good morning. May I help you?

B : Hi, I'm going to check out now. Will you make out my bill?

A : May I have your name and room number?

B : Jeeny Lee, 257.

A : It comes to $336 ma'am. How would you like to pay?

B : I'd like to pay by Visa.

A : Would you give me your credit card and passport, please?

B : Here you are.

A : Would you sign here?
Here is your receipt.
I hope you enjoyed your stay with us, ma'am.

B : I really enjoyed my stay here.

A : I'm very glad to hear that and we look forward to serving you sometime next.

B : Thank you.

Dialogue 4

A : Guest, B : Bellman

A : I'm going to leave now.
Would you send someone up to my room 1002 for my baggage?

B : I'll be right there.
(Knocking on the door) Bellman.

A : Please, come in.
Take these two baggages down to the front desk.

B : Is there anything I can do for you?

A : No thanks.

PART 3

INSIDE KOREA

INSIDE KOREA

44

Taegukki

Taegukki is the national flag of Korea. The design is complex with philosophical significance. The white background symbolizes peace. The red and blue circle in the center called "Taeguk" symbolizes the universe and each divided part makes a perfect balance between the negative and positive power.

According to oriental philosophy, the universe consists of two powers, positive and negative. These are called 'Eum' and 'Yang' in Korea. 'Eum'(blue), negative power, stands for the earth, the moon, the night, water, woman and etc. 'Yang'(red), positive power means the sky, the sun, the day, fire, man and so on.

The Korean national flag represents the Eum-Yang theory. There are the black bars at the corners of the flag. The bars in the upper left corner stand for heaven, those in the lower left earth, those in the upper right water and those in the lower right fire.

INSIDE KOREA

Sijang, Outdoor Market

Dongdaemun(the East Gate) Market is the biggest outdoor market in Asia. You name it and you can get it at the market! The market is open two times a day, from 10 a.m. to 6 p.m. for retailers and shoppers, and from midnight to 4 a.m. for wholesales. Another big market is the South Gate market.

These days western style supermarkets are being introduced to Korea from America, France and Japan. Most of them are discount markets and factory outlets. Especially in satellite cites, most people go shopping at these big westernized shopping malls. Gradually, the traditional Korean market is losing its competitiveness.

INSIDE KOREA

45

I like a son.

Koreans have strong family relationship. Young people live with their parents until they get married. so family members naturally get together for meetings, parties and to discuss family matters. If Koreans have no children, it is a big family concern. But Koreans have different ideas about adoption. That's why Korean orphans have been adopted abroad. After modernization, the number of unmarried young mothers has increased, but only a few families want to adopt children. although they adopt a child, they do it in secret. Sometimes mothers who want to adopt pretend to the pregnant. It is because they try to protect their adopted children from unnecessary problems while they are growing up. Koreans think that the blood line is very important and this is why Koreans prefer to adopt children from their relatives rather than from strangers.

The Korean government has tried to encourage domestic adoption, but failed. Until now Korea has remained a country which exports orphans. It is a pity, but it is not easy to break tradition and custom.

Every family wants at least on boy, so if a young married couple doesn't have a son, they will have a problem. If the husband is the eldest son, the problem becomes serious. That is why we sometimes see large families. If a family has three daughters and no sons, sometimes the third daughter's name is a boy's name because the family expected a boy next.

Since nuclear families have increased, boys outnumber girls because young couples who want a boy have abortions at clinics if the baby's sex is female. This is why the ultrasound exam is banned by the government. When these boys grow up, Korea might need to import women from other countries. The government runs campaigns to break the boy preference custom. One funny slogan is "A good daughter can beat ten boys." which is true.

Mothers and daughters have a strong relationship in Korea even after marriage. So there are some funny sayings such as "If you have a son you will have a domestic trip, but if you have a daughter you will have an overseas trip."

INSIDE KOREA

Singing room

There are places called singing rooms in Korea. They are very different from Karaoke rooms in Japan. Singing rooms have 10 to 20 private rooms, and no alcohol is served.

Each room is equipped with a video monitor which is connected to a melody machine and microphones. Koreans like to go to singing rooms with their family members and friends and take turns singing songs. The Cost is between 8,000 and 15,000 won. People pay it in advance for an hour. Many people practice there favorite songs in these singing rooms.

INSIDE KOREA

46

I had my eyes done.

Creating a fold in the eyelid is the most popular cosmetic surgery among Korean women, Native Westerners have a natural fold, but Oriental people do not. They have more fat in their eyelids than Western people. If Korean women have plastic surgery, their eyes look bigger.

Another popular operation is a nose enlargement. Even young men have this operation to try to look better for job interviews.

The funny thing is that there are some Western people who have operations to make their noses smaller.

INSIDE KOREA

Touch culture

One of the surprising things foreigners experience in Korea is that they get touched or bumped in crowded places. Most Koreans don't worry about touching or bumping into strangers on the street. Some foreigners complain about it. Why don't Koreans say "sorry!" or "Excuse me!" when they touch or bump others? One main reason is that Koreans have been living as one race and they are not used to other races.

Another reason is that Seoul has become one of the busiest cities in the world due to rapid growth. If Koreans sad 'I'm sorry.' whenever they touch others, they would have to say this dozens of times a day.

Koreans become accustomed to this 'touch culture' in childhood. Kids always walk hand in hand with their parents, arm in arm with close friends. Also many Korean women do the same when they walk with their female friends. Dancing with the same sex is very normal in Korea. These are some of the most curious things for some Westerners. Of course most of them are not homosexual.

INSIDE KOREA

47

Life begins at 60.

When Koreans turn 61 years old, they have a big celebration. all family members prepare their parents' 61st birthday. It is called 'Hwan-gap' in Korean. All the sons' and daughters' friends, relatives and neighbours are invited to the party. It is the biggest event in a Korean's life. According to Oriental philosophy, 60 years means one has completed a full zodiac cycle. So Koreans believe they start their lives again at the age of 60. One zodiac circle takes 12 years, and a cycle is completed after 5 circles. At the time of completion, you are reborn.

INSIDE KOREA

Kum-jull, forbidding rope

In the past, when a baby was born, a straw rope called 'Kum-jull' was hung across the front gate for 21 days. In the case of a boy, pieces of charcoal and red peppers were hung on the straw rope. In the case of a girl, family members put charcoal and green pine branches on the straw rope.

They believed that charcoal purified and sterilized the air and kept the baby and mother from infection and gave notice to visitors. No guests were allowed for 21days except close relatives. They believed that the Birth Grandmother would become angry and harm a newborn baby when outsiders frequented the house. nowadays, babies are born in maternity hospitals, so this custom has disappeared.

INSIDE KOREA

48

Wedding

Usually a Korean wedding ceremony is held at a private wedding hall. It is conducted by the bride or bridegroom's teacher or a distinguished person. When Koreans are invited to a wedding ceremony, they prepare a white envelope with money in it. Marriage gifts are not common except very close friends. Most of the guests give a white money envelope to a receptionist at the wedding. The host makes a make list of all the people who give an envelope. If the host is invited to weddings of sons or daughters of guests, the same amount of money is usually give to them.

Weddings are big family events so Koreans give this 'congratulation money' to help pay for the expenses. Sometimes it costs a lot of money for salaried workers especially when there are many weddings during the wedding season. Another occasion for giving a white envelope with money in it is when people die.

There is a special job related to marriage. It is called matchmaker. Matchmakers are middle-aged women who connect daughters of the rich with promising young men like lawyers and doctors. If the couple gets married. the matchmaker receives big commissions from both families. Matchmakers have name lists of hundreds of young people. Of course, it is a tax-free business.

INSIDE KOREA

First birthday party

A Party is held on the 100th day after birth. Koreans believe that if they wish something for 100 days with all their heart, their wishes will come true. So Koreans believe that if the baby survives for 100 days, he will enjoy a long life.

There is also a big celebration on the first birthday of the child. The relatives and friends of the parents are all invited. There is a funny custom on the party day. Parents put thread, a pencil and money on the party table. If the baby picks up the thread, it is said the child will have a long life. A pencil means the child will be a good scholar and money symbolizes a rich man in the future.

When Koreans are invited to the first birthday of a child, they present a gold ring to the parents. Friends and colleagues collect money to buy the gold ring. Some people get many rings. but it is not for the child's finger but for the benefit of the child, in times of need in the future.

PART 4

DICTATION

Dialogue 1

CHAPTER 1
RESERVATION

1

C : Reservation Clerk

P : Passenger

C : Asiana Airlines. Can I help you?

P : I want to ____________ to Manila the day after tomorrow.

C : Yes, Ma'am. What time would you like to fly?

P : Is there a flight early in the morning?

C : Yes, there is. We have a ____ at 8 a.m.

P : I'll take that.

C : O.K. May I have your name, please?

P : Lucy Lee.

C : May I have your __________, please?

P : The number is 031-205-6732.

C : O.K. Your ________ has been made for flight 701 leaving for Manila on Aug. 13, Sunday at 7 a.m. Your reservation number is C67576. Thank you for calling Asiana Airlines.

P : Thank you Bye.

Dialogue 2

C : Good morning. Ha-na Travel ______.

This is Ms. Park speaking.

How May I help you?

P : Good morning. I'm ____________ to New York this winter and was wondering if you could give me some information ____________.

C : Sure. When do you want to travel?

P : Anytime on Jan. 1st. How much is a ____________ to New York?

C : Do you have any airline you prefer?

P : Not really.

C : Well, Fly Airline Offers 1,100,000 won for a round-trip ticket to JFK. It's a __________.

P : Wow, that's pretty ________. Do you have any lower rates?

C : Well, The cheapest one we have is one million won, World Airline.

P : That sounds better.

Dialogue 3

2

C : Good afternoon. May I help you?

P : Do you have a flight from Incheon to LA on May 5th?

C : When would you ___________?

P : In the afternoon May 5th.

C : You have to change ____________. That one is booked.

P : When is the next flight?

C : How about the 8 p.m. flight, ma'am?

P : 8 o'clock in the evening? That's _______. I'll take that one.

C : Please be sure to check-in at the airport ________________ before your flight time.

Dialogue 4

C : But it's not a __________. It stops over in Tokyo.

P : That doesn't matter. How many flights does it have daily?

C : They have ______________, one at 3:30 p.m. and another at 8:00 p.m.

P : I'd better take the earlier one. When does it arrive in New York?

C : It arrives in New York at 4:40 p.m. ______________. When would you like to return?

P : Can I leave it open?

C : Of course, you can. Are you a student?

P : Yes. My sister and I are both students.

C : __________, I Can give you a student discount. That's 20% off. So that'll be 800,000 won for each.

P : Great! That's even better. Could you book me on that?

Dialogue 5

C : World Airline reservation. How can I help you?

P : Hi, I'd like to ____________________.

C : Can I have your ________, please?

P : My last name is Kim and my first name is Mi-Ae. I'm travelling with my brother.

C : Could you tell me _________________?

P : Oh, I have the reservation number. Would it be any help?

C : Oh, sure. Please go ahead.

P : It's CBCD2F.

CHAPTER 2
CONFIRMATION

Dialogue 1

3

P : Hello, Is this the Ana Airlines __________?

C : Yes, it is. May I help you?

P : I need to ______ my reservation to Tokyo.

C : O.K., sir. Your name, please?

P : Daniel Jackson.

C : Your reservation is confirmed in economy class. Your ________ ___ is 7:30 a.m.

P : Is that direct flight?

C : Sure.

P : When can I receive the ticket?

C : You can ______ your ticket tomorrow through e-mail.

P : Can I send my payment on line or by credit card?

C : Either is fine.

P : What credit cards ____________?

C : Any major credit card will be fine.

P : Very well. Thank you.

Dialogue 2

C : Would you hold the line ___________?

P : Yes.

C : Thank you for waiting, Miss Kim. You're flying to New York on Flight 179, economy class, ________ 3:30 p.m. on Jan. 1st. Right?

P : Correct.

C : OK, your reservation is confirmed. Your confirmation number is the same as your reservation number.

P : Is that all?

C : One more thing. Will you please ________ two hours prior to the departure time?

P : OK, I will. But why is that?

C : You have to check in for the flight and go through immigration. It takes about that time.

P : I see. Thanks for your help.

C : Thank you for calling. Have a nice trip!

Dialogue 3

C : Good morning. Korean Airlines reservation. Can I help you?

P : I'd like to ____________________ on flight 397 for the 13 of next month.

C : Oh, I see. Can I have your name, please?

P : Daniel Lee.

C : One moment please, Mr. Lee.

(Pause)

Thank you for waiting, sir. Now your reservation is cancelled.

Do you want to make a _____________?

P : No, I haven't _________________ yet.

C : All right, sir. Thank you for calling.

Please, call us again _________ you want to make a new reservation. Good-bye, sir.

Dialogue 1

CHAPTER 3
TICKETING

4 A : Airline counter

P : Passenger

A : Good afternoon, ma'am. What can I help you with?

P : I'd like to buy an __________ LA.

A : Would you like ________ or round trip?

P : I want a ______________, please.

A : What flight do you want to take?

P : I'll take the earliest flight possible.

Dialogue 2

A : Good morning. How may I help you?

P : Yes, I made a reservation for a flight to Tokyo on Saturday.

A : May I have your name, ma'am?

P : My name is Jannet smith.

A : You are going to Tokyo OZ 102, ____________, aren't you?
It is $1050 for the round trip, Ms. Smith.

P : ____________ card do you accept?

A : We _________________ credit cards.

P : Do you accept Visa card, too?

A : Sure. May I have your card and _______?

P : Here you are.

A : Would you please sign here, Ms. Smith?

P : Sure.

A : Do you need anything else?

P : No, that's all.

Dialogue 1

CHAPTER 4
CHECK IN SERVICE

5

A : Airline agent

P : Passenger

A : Good evening, sir. May I see your ticket and passport?

P : ____________.

A : Do you have any baggage to check in?

P : Yes. I have two _______ and one golf club bag.

A : Would you put your baggage __________?

P : O.K. Can you put a fragile tag on my suitcases?

A : All right. Here are your ________________ and boarding pass, sir. Have a nice flight!

P : Thanks a lot.

Dialogue 2

A : Good morning. Can I have your ticket and passport, please?

P : Here you are.

A : Would you like an ______________________?

P : I prefer an aisle seat please.

I want to go to lavatory without ________ another passenger during the flight.

A : O.K. I see.

Do you have __________ to check in?

P : Yes. one.

A : Could you put your baggage on the scale, please?

P : All right.

A : Here are your boarding pass and baggage claim tag.

Your seat is 35c and the boarding Gate is 27.

P : Thank you so much.

A : You're welcome. Enjoy your trip.

Dialogue 3

6 A : Hello. ______________ to San Francisco today?

P : Yes, I have my e-ticket.

A : Great. I need to see your passport as well.

P : Here you are.

A : I'll check.

Great. Here you are.

P : Would I be able to ___________ seat?

A : Sure.

P : Thanks.

A : Are you just checking these bags?

P : Yes, I'll take my backpack as my carry-on.

A : Anything fragile in your bags?

P : No.

A : Okay. Here is your boarding pass. Be at the gate one hour prior to boarding time.

Dialogue 4

A : Would you _____ a window or an aisle seat?

P : Which one is better?

A : That depends. Some people like to look at the clouds during the flight. But, the window seats are harder to get in and out of.

P : I'll take the aisle, then.

Dialogue 5

P : Do I check in here for World Airline Flight 179 to New York?

A : Yes. Do you ______ have your tickets?

P : Yes. Here you are.

A : Thank you. May I see your passports, too?

P : Sure. Can I have a __________, please?

A : Let's see. Good. We have seat 12H and 12K. Do you have __________ to check in?

P : Yes, we have two suitcases and one carry-on.

A : Is your name and address on your bag. ma'am?

P : Yes, it is.

A : Can you put your luggage up here, please?

P : OK.

Dialogue 6

7

A : Here are __________ and your boarding passes. Flight 272 to Seattle. Seat 12H and 12K. It departs from Gate 11 at 3:20. Enjoy your flight!

P1 : Thank you. Could __________ where departure gate 11 is, please?

A : Yes. Just take the ________ up to the next level and turn right. All the gates are upstairs.

P2 : Thanks.

P1 : Is it possible to buy ________ and gifts here?

A : Yes. Go to level 2. Look for the duty-free shop in the ____________. It's near the telephones. You can't miss it. You'll find lots of famous brands there.

P2 : Thanks for the help.

Dialogue 7

Getting on board

Announcement : Passengers for Seattle, may I have your ______. please? World Airline's Flight 272 to Seattle, __________ depart at 3:30, has been delayed due to late arrival from Tokyo. Flight 272 will now depart at 3:50 from Gate 11. Boarding will begin in 15 minutes.

Dialogue 8

Announcement : Good afternoon. World Airline Flight 179 departing at 3:50 for JFK Airport in New York City is now __________ at Gate 11. Passengers with small children or who require special help in boarding, please proceed to Gate 11, now. The Flight is 20 minutes ______________ and will depart at 3:50 p.m. now. Sorry for the delay. Next, all those passengers in rows 39 through 56, please board.

(on the plane)

C : Good afternoon, ma'am. What's your seat number?
P : Uh, it's 12K.
C : That's on the left side of the airplane. It's by the window.
P : Thank you.

Dialogue 1

8

C : Cabin Attendant

P : Passenger

C : Good morning, sir. ________________.

P : Good morning. Where is 43G.

C : Please ____ the other aisle.

Your seat is in the back of the cabin.

P : Thanks.

C : You're welcome, sir.

Dialogue 2

P : Excuse me. Where is my seat?

C : It's over there 33B, your seat is _______________ the cabin on your right.

P : Thank you.

C : Anytime, ma'am. Have a nice flight.

Dialogue 3

P : Excuse me. miss.

Where can I put my bag? It's too big. And I ____________ _____ for it.

C : Would you like me to keep your bag in the coatroom?

P : Please. Thank you.

C : It's my pleasure.

C : Excuse me, ma'am. Is this your bag?

P : Yes, why?

C : I'm sorry. ma'am.

Would you please ___________ the seat in front of you.

We must _____ the aisle clear.

P : All right.

C : Thank you very much.

C : Excuse me, sir.

Would you mind ________ under the seat?

It might fall during turbulence.

Dialogue 4

9 C : Good morning. ma'am.

May I see your ____________, please?

P : Here you are.

C : Your ___________ is 37B. It's on your right side.

May I help you with your bag?

P : Here you are.

C : Thank you.

C : Excuse me. ma'am. May I help you?

P : No. I'm ____________.

C : Would you please take your seat during boarding?

P : Okay, I'll sit.

C : Thank you, ma'am.

C : Excuse me, sir. May I help you?

P : No. I'm looking around.

C : Would you please _________ to let these people through?

P : Okay, I'll sit.

C : Thank you, sir.

Dialogue 5

C : Good morning, ma'am. May I help you ______________?

P : Yes, please. Oh, thank you, sir.

C : Come this way, please. This is your seat.

Please keep this bag in the ____________.

P : May I have some water?

C : I will get it for you after everyone has _______, ma'am.

(Pause)

Here's your water, ma'am.

P : Thank you.

CHAPTER 6
SEATING

Dialogue 1

10

P1 : Excuse me, miss. ________________ on my seat.

C : May I see your boarding pass, please?

Thank you.

(to P2) Excuse me, sir.

May I see your boarding pass, please?

Thank you, sir.

__________ I'm afraid you might be in the wrong seat.

Your seat is over there.

Would you please _____ seats?

I'll help you with your bags.

P2 : Oh, all right.

C : (to P1) Thank you for waiting, sir.

Dialogue 2

P : Do you have any empty seats in front of the cabin

C : Would you please wait ____ everyone has boarded. sir?

I'll check it for you later.

(Pause)

C : We have some ___________ in the front of the cabin.

(Move to the front seat)

Would you like to sit there?

P : Can I move __________ the cabin. I think there are empty seats.

C : Would you please wait until everyone has boarded, sir?

Let me _______ for you later.

(Pause)

C : I'm sorry.

All the seats are ________ today.

Dialogue 3

11

P1 : Miss, there's someone _________.

C : (to both)

May I see your boarding pass, please?

Thank you

I'm afraid there was a ______ in the arrangement of seats.

(to P1)

Come this way please.

Would you please wait here?

I will check it _________.

Just a moment, please.

(to P1)

Thank you for waiting sir. Your seat is _________.

This way, please.

Here you are.

I'm sorry for the inconvenience.

Dialogue 4

P : Excuse me, my son and I were _______ separate seats.
Do you have any __________ together?

C : Oh, I'll check. We have some seats in the middle of the cabin. Would that be alright?

P : That's good. thank you.

C : May I help you with your bags?

P : No, thank you. ___________.

C : Come this way, please.
Have a pleasant flight.

P : Excuse me, my wife and I were assigned separate seats.
Do you have any empty seats together?

C : I'm sorry, sir. But after take-off, I'll come back and let you know.

(after take off)

I'm sorry, sir. But __________ are occupied today.

Is there anything else I can do for you?

P : Oh, No. Thank you. that's all.

Dialogue 5

P : My colleagues are sitting over there, and we want to sit together.
Can I change my seat?

C : I'll check after everyone __________ and let you know.

(after boarding)

Thanks for waiting, I have found some seats for you.

Come this way please.

Dialogue 1

CHAPTER 7
GROUND SERVICE

12

Newspaper service

C : Would you like to ________________, sir?

P : I'll have the Cho-sun Il-bo.

C : Sure. Here you are.

C : Would you care for a newspaper, ma'am?

P : Do you have Newsweek?

C : I'm sorry, ma'am.

Newsweek is not _______ in this flight.

Would you like the Korea Times, instead?

Earphone service

C : Here are your _________, sir.

P : Thank you

When are you going to _____________?

C : We'll be showing the movie in about 2 hours.

Dialogue 2

Mother with a baby

C : We prepared some __________ you need.

We have diapers, baby food, ___________ and bottles.

If you need anything, please let me know.

P : All right. Thank you so much.

C : You're welcome, ma'am.

C : Would you like to ______________ for your baby?

P : Yes, I'd like to.

C : I'll set up a bassinet after take-off.

P : Thank you.

Dialogue 3

C : Excuse me, ma'am.

P1 : Yes?

C : Let me put that bag in the ____________________ for you.
It's too big to leave under your seat.

P1 : Oh, OK. Thanks.

P2 : Excuse me. Could you please help me close this overhead compartment?
I can't _________.

C : Sure. Let me try.

P2 : Thank you.

Dialogue 1

13

C : (notice that a passenger does not have his seatbelt fastened)

Excuse me, sir. Please _____ your seatbelt now.

We will be taking off _____. Thank you.

C : (To a child who is too small for the seatbelt)

Here, let me put this _____ under your seatbelt.

It will be more comfortable that way.

P : Thank you.

P : I don't like _______ my seatbelt.

C : I'm sorry, but I must ask you to fasten. Your seatbelt for take-off.

P : I'll just need to _______ my friend over there.

C : I understand. But, it's an Airline Regulations.

C : Excuse me.

Could you please close your tray table until after take-off?

Thank you.

C : I'm sorry, sir, but you'll need to return your chair and tray table to their ______________ for takeoff.

P : How do I get my chair to go back up?

I think it's stuck.

C : There's a __________ on the side of the armrest. Press it and lean forward.

Dialogue 2

About restroom use

P : Excuse me. Can I use the _______ now?

C : I'm afraid not now, sir. Could you wait until after taking off, please?

We will be taking off shortly.

P : Hello. Can I go to the lavatory?

C : Yes, but please hurry up. We'll be taking off soon.

P : OK, then, I'll use the lavatory after take off.

Dialogue 1

14

Towel Distribution

C : Would you like a ________, ma'am?

It's very hot. Please be careful.

Towel Pick up

C : Are you _______ with your towel, ma'am?

P : Yes, I am. Thank you.

C : (Taking the towel) You're welcome.

If the passenger is sleeping

C : (Quietly and gently) Excuse me, sir.

Would you like a hot towel?

We'll be serving _______ soon.

Headset service

C : Here's your ______ ma'am.

P : No, thanks. I don't want to buy one.

C : Our headsets are ____________.

P : In that case, I'll have it. thanks.

Movie information request

C : Here's your headset, ma'am.

P : Thank you. What ______ are you showing today?

C : Today's movies are G I Joe. and Public Enemy.

P : Excuse me. When are you _______ the movie?

C : About an hour later.

Dialogue 2

C : Would you carre for something to drink?

P : Yes, I'll have some juice.

P : What ___________ do you have?

C : We have orange, pineapple, tomato and guava juice, sir.

P : I'll have orange juice.

C : ________, sir.

(to the next passenger)

And you, ma'am?

P : May I have a Gin & Tonic?

C : I'm sorry, ma'am.

I'm _____ we don't serve Gin on this flight.

P : Oh, I see.

I'll have some water, then.

Dialogue 3

15

Suggesting a cocktail

C : Excuse me, sir. Would you like something to drink? We have juice, cocktails, ______ and beer on this flight.

P : I want cocktails. What do you have?

C : We have Manhattan, Martini, Sloe Gin and others. Which one do you prefer?

P : Nothing in ________.

C : If you like something weak, how about a bloody mary?

P : All right. Let me try it.

C : Here you go, sir. Enjoy your drink.

Dialogue 4

Request for another round(Drink)

P : Excuse me. Could I have another drink?

C : You were _______ a Gin & Tonic, weren't you?

P : Yes, that's right.

C : Just a moment, please. Here you are.

Beverage service : Pick up

C : Excuse me, sir. Are you finished with your drink?

P : Yes, I'm ______.

C : May I ____________?

P : Sure, you will.

C : Thank you, sir.

Beverage service : Weak or strong drink

P : Excuse me. My coffee is ______ strong.

C : I'm sorry, sir. Let me change it.

P : Thank you.

Dialogue 5

16 **Meal service (short portion)**

C : We are now about to _____ lunch, ma'am.

Would you please open your tray table?

P : What's the meal today?

C : We only have _______ today.

P : I don't like seafood.

C : I'm sorry, ma'am.

We only offer seafood on this flight.

P : Well, __________________ anyway.

C : Here you are, ma'am.

I hope you enjoy your meal.

Dialogue 6

Meal service : on a long flight

C : Please return your seat to the upright position.

We are serving __________ for this flight?

P1 : Fish, please.

C : Please open your tray table.

Here you are. _____________ and enjoy your meal.

P2 : I'd like the beef, please.

C : (to T3) How about you, ma'am?

Dialogue 7

17

Meal service : Entree runs out

C : Excuse me, here is your meal, sir.

P : What kind of meal is this?

C : It's Korean style beef.

P : Well, I ____________ very much. I'd like the chicken, please.

C : I'm sorry sir, but we _________ chicken today. Now we only have beef left.

P : All right. I'll take the beef then.

C : Here you are. I apologize for not being able to _____ you the chicken.

We will start to serve from the back of the cabin, so, you can surely have __________ on the next serve.

P : That's great. I'll be waiting then.

Dialogue 8

Special request meal

P : Miss, I ________ a vegetarian meal.

C : I see. sir. I'll check it for you right away.

Just a moment, please.

(Pause)

C : Thank you for waiting.

Here you are. Enjoy your meal, sir.

C : Excuse me, sir.

Did you ______ a Kosher meal?

P : Yes, I did.

C : Here is your meal.

May I open your meal?

P : Yes, please.

Dialogue 9

18

Special meal not requested

C : Which on would you like beef or fish, sir?

P : Are there any ___________ for me? I don't like beef and I'm allergic to fish.

C : I'm sorry but, I'm afraid you Should have _______ a special meal _______ two days before the flight departure.

P : Oh, I didn't know that. I'll try to do it next time.

C : I'm sorry, sir.

Dialogue 10

Drink service during the meal

C : Would you care for some coffee or tea?

P : No thanks. Could I have another beer, ______?

C : Certainly. Here you are. Enjoy your meal.

(To next passenger) What about you ma'am?

Would you like __________ wine?

P2 : Yes, please. That would be great.

C : Here you are.

C : Coffee or tea, ma'am?

P : I'll have some tea please.

And could I ______________ for my son.

C : Certainly, ma'am. May I have your cup, please?

Thank you. Here's your tea and milk.

P : Thank you very much.

C : My pleasure ma'am. Enjoy your meal.

Dialogue 11

19

Wine service

C : Would you like some wine _________ your salmon?

P : Yes, please.

C : Which would you _____, red or white wine?

P : White, please.

C : Here you are.

P : Thank you.

Wine Service : refill

P : Can I have some more wine?

C : Did you have white wine?

P : Yes, I did. Thank you.

Dialogue 12

Meal tray pick-up

C : Excuse me, sir.

Are ______________ your meal?

P : Yes, I am.

C : May I take your meal tray?

P : Of course.

C : Did you enjoy your meal. sir?

P : Yes, It was ________.

C : Are you _______ with your meal?

P : No, I'm not finished yet.

C : I'm sorry, ma'am.

Please ______________ and enjoy your meal.

P : Thank you.

C : Would you like some more coffee or tea?

P : I want some coffee, please.

C : I'll ________________ right away.

Just a moment, please.

Here you are.

Dialogue 13

20

In-flight sales : Shopping guide

C : Would you like to buy any __________?

P : __________ items do you have?

C : Here is the shopping guide. sir.

C : Would you like to buy something, sir?

P : Yes, what do you have?

C : Here is the __________. It will help you with the items we have.

P : Thank you.

Dialogue 14

In-flight sales : (General)

C : Would you like to ____________?

P : Could I have ____________ Dunhill and _________ Chivas Regal, please.

C : Certainly. Here you are. That will be $150, please.

P : Here you are.

C : Would you like to buy something from the duty free?

P : Could I have ____________ Kent and a bottle of Ballentine's 17 years old, please.

C : Certainly. here you are. __________ $170, please.

P : Do you accept cards?

C : Yes, We do.

C : Here's your change, ma'am.

P : Keep the change.

C : Thank you. But we are not allowed to ________.

Dialogue 15

21

Sold Out

C : Would you like to buy any duty free items?

P : Yes, I'd like __________ old parr, please.

C : I'm sorry, but it's ________.

Would you like another items instead?

Dialogue 16

In–flight sales : Change not available

P : Excuse me. All I have is a 100 dollar bill. Do you have any change?

C : I'm sorry, sir. I'm afraid I don't ____________ right now, but I'll ________________________.

(Pause)

Thank you for waiting.

Here is your change, sir.

P : Thank you.

Dialogue 17

Acceptable currency

C : Here you are. That will be 40 dollars, sir.

P : I don't have any dollars. ______________ thailand baht?

C : I'm sorry, sir. I am afraid we do not accept Thailand Baht. Do you have ________________?

P : I have some Korean won.

C : That'll be fine, sir.

Dialogue 18

Document Service : Entering Korea

22

P : Miss. I'm a tourist.

C : Yes, sir.

All ________ entering Korea must fill out the ED card and the

____________.

P : I see.

Do you have an English form for customs?

C : Yes, sir.

Here you are, sir.

Dialogue 19

Entering the U.S.A.

P : Do I need these cards?

C : Are you a U.S. ______________?

P : Yes, I'm a U.S. citizen.

C : Then you only need customs form.

C : Are you a U.S. citizen or a resident?

P : No, I'm german.

C : Then you'll need the entry card and the __________.

P : Do I need these cards?

I live in the U.S., but I'm not a ________.

C : Do you have an alien registration card?

P : Yes, I do.

C : Then you only need the ________________, sir.

Dialogue 20

23 C : Excuse me, sir. Are you an ____________?

P : No, I'm not.

C : Do you have a visa for the United States?

P : Yes, I do.

C : Could you fill out this entry card before we arrive, please? It's for ________.

P : All right.

C : Thank you.

P : Oh, I ______ bring something to write with. Do you have a pen?

C : Here you are.

Dialogue 21

Questions from Passengers : Flight time

P : How long __________ to Los Angeles?

C : Our scheduled flight time will be 9 hours and 20 minutes today.

P : What's the ______________ between Seoul & Los Angeles?

C : Seoul is 16 hours ahead of Los Angeles.

P : I see. thank you.

C : You're welcome, sir.

Dialogue 22

Arrival Time

C : Would you like some coffee, sir?

P : Yes, that will be great.

By the way, how long will it take to Honolulu?

C : We ________________ 3 hours from now.

P : I see. Thank you.

Dialogue 23

24 **No Time difference**

P : May I ____________?

C : Yes, you may.

P : What's the time difference between Seoul and Narita?

C : There is no time difference between these two cities.

Time difference

P : How much is the time difference between Seoul and New York?

C : There is a _______________ between Seoul and New York. New York is 14 hours behind Seoul.

Dialogue 24

Turbulence

C : Could you fasten your seatbelt, sir?

P : Excuse me?

C : The pilots ________ the fasten seatbelt sign.

We may be having some turbulence.

P : Oh, really? ____________, I hope.

C : I hope not. Oops.

P : Excuse me. Could I have a ____________ card?

I can't find one in the seat pocket.

C : Let me get you one.

P : Can I use the lavatory?

C : Sorry. You aren't allowed to leave your seat right now.

Dialogue 25

25 C : Ma'am, you're free to get up and walk around the cabin. now.

The ______________ has been turned off.

P1 : Good. Thank you.

P2 : Excuse me. It's very chilly in here. Do you have an extra blanket?

C : Yes, I'll bring you a blanket.

P2 : By the way. What's our ETA?

C : We were due in at 5:00 p.m., but I think we're going to be late.

P1 : Will you ________________ for duty-free items?

C : Yes. I'll back in a minute.

Dialogue 26

Sick Passenger

(Pax call chimes)

C : Yes, ma'am, May I help you?

P : Yes, I have a ________________.

Do you have some medicine?

C : I'm sorry, to hear that, ma'am.

We have Tylenol on board.

Are you __________ any medicine?

P : No. I am not.

C : I see, I'll get some for you right away.

(pause)

C : Here you are. I hope you will feel better soon.

P : Thank you.

Dialogue 27

26

Medicine for airsick

P : Excuse me, miss. I _________ very easily.

I feel ____.

Do you have anything for that?

C : I'm sorry to hear that, sir. We have bonamin.

Would that be alright?

P : Yes, that's alright.

C : Just a moment, please.

(pause)

C : I hope you feel better.

Dialogue 28

Medicine for indigestion

P : Excuse me, miss. Do you have anything for indigestion?

C : Yes, sir. We have Festal on board.

Are you allergic to any ________?

P : No, I am not.

C : I'll get one for you ____.

(Pause)

C : Here you are. I hope you get well soon.

Dialogue 29

NO SMOKING

C : Excuse me, sir.

Smoking ______________ during the entire flight.

P : Oh, I am sorry.

C : Thank you.

Dialogue 1

CHAPTER 10
PREPARATION FOR LANDING

27 P : Excuse me, Miss. May I have some coffee, please?

C : I'm sorry, sir. We've ________________.

P : No, I don't mind at all.

C : Thank you. sir.

Dialogue 2

C : Excuse me, sir. We'll be landing at Inchon international airport shortly.

Can I ______________________, please?

P : Here is it. Would you take this used cup?

C : Thank you.

P : You're welcome.

Dialogue 3

C : Could you put your seat ______ now, ma'am?
We'll be ____________.

P : So soon? great.

C : And I'm also collecting the headsets. Would you mind passing them to me, please?

P : No problem. Here you go.

Dialogue 4

28 C : Excuse me, sir.

Did you fasten your seatbelt? We'll be landing shortly.

Thank you.

C : Would you please return your seat ______________?

P : I see.

C : Would you mind closing your tray table, too?

We'll be landing soon.

C : Excuse me, ma'am.

Would you please ___________ under the seat until after landing?

It might fall out during landing.

P : O.K.

Dialogue 5

Returning passenger's personal belongings

P : Would you bring me the bag I ______________?

C : Yes, sir. I'll be right back.

(pause)

Here you are.

P : Thank you.

C : You're welcome, sir.

I hope to see you on board again soon.

CHAPTER 11
FAREWELL AND DEPLANING

Dialogue 1

29 During taxiing

P : (Standing and getting bags from overhead during taxiing)

C : Excuse me. Would you please __________ until the plane completely stops?

It's for your safety.

P : Oh, I'm sorry.

Dialogue 2

Saying good-bye : farewell

C : Good-bye, sir. ______________________ Asiana Airlines. We hope to see you on board again.

P : Good-bye. I enjoyed flight.

C : Have a good trip in Seoul.

CHAPTER 1
HOTEL RESERVATION

Dialogue 1

30

A : Tour Counselor, B : Guest

A : Good afternoon. Lucy Travel Agency, may I help you?

B : Yes. I'm planning a business trip to LA for 6 days from June 4th. Can you __________ a good hotel downtown?

A : Yes. We have several deluxe hotels located in downtown.

B : How can I get to the hotel from the airport? This is my first visit to LA and I have ___ __ baggages.

A : Don't worry, sir. If you want, the hotel will _______ limousine service to ____ ___ __.

B : How far is the hotel from the airport?

A : It _______ __ traffic congestion in the city, but usually it'll take about 1 hour by car.

B : Please fix me up with a room at the Star hotel for 6 nights from _____ ___ and also arrange pick up service for me at the airport.

A : O.K. We'll _______ a room and ___________ for you when you arrive in LA. And would you fill up this travel request form, please?

B : Sure... Here you go.

Dialogue 2

A : Desk Clerk, B : Caller

A : Seoul Hotel. How may I help you?

B : Yes. Do you have any rooms ________ for tomorrow?

A : Let's see.
We have some rooms ________ tomorrow.
Would you like a single or a double?

B : Are there any deluxe _____ available?

A : I'm sorry, all deluxe suites are ____ booked.
How would you like a double room with a ____ ____?

B : What's the room like?

A : It's on the 3rd floor ___________ a fine view of Mt. Namsan.
It's also a very quiet room.

B : That sounds good.

Dialogue 3

31

A : Desk Clerk, B : Guest, C : Reservation Clerk

A : Hello, Pacific Hotel. Can I help you?

B : Yes, I need to make a room __________.

A : _____ __, please. I'll connect you with our reservation department.

C : Reservation office, how may I help you?

B : Can I _____ a room in your hotel for 5 ______ from May 10th?

C : Just a moment, sir. I'll check if there is any room available. I'm sorry, sir. All rooms are ________ except suit rooms. Would that be all right, sir?

B : What's a suite?

C : It's a more spacious room. It comes with ________ living room and bed room.

B : Sounds great. But it must be very _________.

C : Compared to regular rooms the _________ is $100 for one day. Would you like me to book for you?

B : Oh, that's too expensive.

C : Then we can put you on the waiting list. Would that be alright?

B : That will be better.

Dialogue 4

A : Reservation Clerk, B : Jeeny Lee

A : Good afternoon. Reservation desk. Kim Speaking.

B : Yes, I'd like to make a reservation.

A : ________________________________?

B : A double with bath.

A : How long would you like to stay?

B : From ______ __ to ______ ____.

A : Would you like a room with an _____ ____ or a ________ ____?

B : With a mountain view, please.

A : We have a room with a nice mountain view of Mt. Namsan.

B : That's very good. I'll take it.

A : May I have your name, please?

B : Yes, Jeeny Lee.

A : I'm ______ _______ to ______ you on August 1st.

B : Thank you. Good Bye.

Dialogue 5

A : Reservation Clerk, B : Jeeny Lee

A : Good morning. Room reservation. Lee speaking. Can I help you?

B : Yes, I'd like to know if I can change my reservation ____ __ ____.

A : May I have your name and your ________ ______ ____, please?

B : My name is Jeeny Lee.
I am ________ to be there on July 20th but I'd like to _____ the arrival date to August 4th. Would that be _______?

A : Just a moment.
I'm _____ but we're ____ _______ on that date.

B : Well, is there any way I could get a room?

A : We can put you on the ______ __ or arrange you at another hotel around here.

B : Please put me on the waiting list.

A : Very well.

Dialogue 1

CHAPTER 2
CHECK-IN

32

A : Bellman, B : Customer

A : Welcome to Namsan Hotel. May I help you with your ________?

B : Yes, please.

A : Do you have any baggage in the _____?

B : Yes, I have 2 more bags in the trunk.

A : O.K., ma'am. I'll _____ _____ you have everything.
Please go ______, I'll bring in your bags.

B : Thank you.

A : You're welcome.

Dialogue 2

A : Bellman, B : Guest

A : Good afternoon. May I help you, sir?

B : Yes, please. I have two baggages in ___ ___ _____.
Would you _____ those baggages to room 556 for me?

A : Yes, sir. ___ ___ _____ your baggages to room 556.

B : Thanks a lot.

A : Please _____ ___ of the ________ ____. The _____ door is ________.

B : Thank you for ______ ___. ___ ___ ___, where can I _______?

A : You can _______ at the front desk ____ ____ _____.

Dialogue 3

33

A : Receptionist, B : Jeeny Lee

A : May I help you, Miss?

B : Yes. I have a reservation.

A : May I have your name?

B : My name is Jeeny Lee.

A : That's ______. Your name doesn't _____ to be here.

B : It could be _____ my father's name, Peter Lee.

A : Yes, we have your reservation under the name of Peter Lee. Would you like to __ ___ this __________ ____?

B : OK... Here you are.

A : Thank you. And you'll be in room 855 – that's on the ____ floor.

B : Thanks for helping.

A : My pleasure.

Dialogue 4

A : Receptionist, B : Bill

A : How may I help you?

B : We don't have a reservation.

Do you have two ______ rooms ________ for tonight?

A : I'm sorry, but _____ rooms are _______ up already.

But we have some ______ rooms left.

B : Are those rooms ____ _ _____ _____?

A : Yes. There are.

B : That's great.

A : Would you like to sign this __________ ____, please?

B : Sure.

A : You will be in room 712 and room 713.

_______ will bring up your luggages.

_____ ____ ____.

B : Thank you.

Dialogue 5

34 *A : Receptionist, B : Mr. and Mrs. Kim*

A : Good afternoon. May I help you?

B : Do you have a room in the name of Mr. and Mrs. Kim?

A : ___ ___ _____. Yes, we do have a reservation for you.

B : I ______ a _____ room but don't you have a ___ room _______?

A : Yes, we do. It has a ___ ___ of Waikiki beach.

B : Well, does the _______ have a ___?

A : Yes, it does have a large tub.

B : That's good. I think that will do.

A : ___ ___ __ ___ ___ __ ___?

B : For 4 days, until the 10th.

A : Alright. Please ___ ___.

Dialogue 6

A : Receptionist, B : Jason Kim

A : Welcome to the Pacific Hotel, sir!
Do you have a reservation ____ __?
B : Yes, we do. My name is Jason Kim.
A : ____ ____ _______, sir... You are Mr. Kim.
B : Yes, that's right.
A : You ________ a ______ room for three nights, didn't you?
B : Yes, I did.
A : Your room is _____, sir. It's number 656, which has a ____ ______ _____. Please fill out this __________ form and I'll ___ your key.
B : OK... Here's the form. Are your restaurants ___ _____?
A : Yes, sir, they are open until 10 p.m. and the coffee shop until 2 a.m.
B : How about the ________ ________?
A : You can use the ______ ____ and ____ anytime you like.
B : That's good.
A : Do you have any _________ that you would like for us to _______ our hotel ____?
B : I guess we don't.
A : Here is your key, and this bellman will _____ your bags to your room.
B : Thanks a lot.
A : _____ ____ ____.

Dialogue 1

35

A : Room Service, B : Guest

A : Good morning, Room service. May I help you?

B : Hello, Are you ______ ______ ______?

A : No, sir. Breakfast menu is until 10:00 a.m.

B : Good. Then, can I have a ______ ______?

A : You have a choice of _____ or ___ ____, sir?

B : Fruit juice, please.

A : ___ ___ __ _____?

B : Coffee please. Also, I want to order two _____ _____ __ with french fries.

A : Anything else?

B : No, thank you.

Dialogue 2

A : Room Service, B : Peter Park

A : Room service, may I help you?

B : Yes. I'd like to have ________ ________ in my room ________ ________.

A : Which do you like ______ juice or ______ juice?

B : Orange juice _____ ___ _____.

A : ____ _____ ___ ___ your eggs?

B : Sunny-side up, please.

A : All right, sir. _____ _____ ___ ___ coffee or tea?

B : Black tea, please.

A : May I have your room number?

B : My name is Peter Park in room 507.

A : ____ ___ _____ ___ ___ _ ______, sir?

B : At 7:30 a.m.

__ ____ they aren't too cold.

A : I'll ____ _ ____ for you.

B : Thank you.

Dialogue 3

36

A : Room Service, B : Guest

A : (knocking on the door) Hello. Room service.

B : _____ __ __.

A : I've _______ your lunch you _______, sir. Where do you want ___ __ ___ _?

B : Over there by the window will be fine.

A : _____ I _____ you a cup of coffee straightaway?

B : No thanks! I'll take care of it.

A : Is there ________ ____ ___ _____?

B : No, I don't think so. Everything is just perfect.

A : _____ ____ _____.

Dialogue 4

A : Waiter, B : Guest

A : Good morning, sir. ____ _ ____ ____ _____ ____?

B : Yes, I'll have American breakfast.

A : _____ _____ _ _____ ___ ____ _____? We have orange, grapefruit, and tomato juice.

B : I'll have a tomato juice.

A : OK, and you also ___ two eggs _______ __ ___ ____.

B : Boiled, please. And I'll have cereals, please.

A : Yes, sir. ______ __ ___?

B : A cup of tea please, with sugar and lemon.

A : All right. _ _____ _____ ____ _____, sir.

Dialogue 5

A : Waiter, B : Guest

A : ___ ___ _____ _ _____ ___?

B : Could we have a few minutes, please?

A : No problem, _____ ____ ___.

(pause)

A : _____ ___ ________ __?

B : Yes. I'll have the grilled chicken breast.

A : ____ _____ _____?

B : What kind of bread do you have?

A : We have ____ and ___ ___.

B : Soft rolls, please.

A : ____ ____ _ ________ ______ ___ ___?

B : Oil and vinegar on the side, please.

A : Would you like some ______ __ ____ _______?

B : Yes, please.

A : I'll have your ______ ________ ______ __ _ ______.

B : Thank you.

Dialogue 6

37

A : Waiter, B : Guest

A : Good evening, ma'am. _____ _ _____ ______.

B : Everything looks good.

A : _____ ______ ____ ____ this evening?

B : I'd like a steak, please.

A : _____ ______ ____ ____ _____ _____?

B : Medium, please. And can I have it with rice instead of potato?

A : And _____ _____ _ _____ ______ ____ ____ _ _____?

B : Well. What's the soup of the day?

A : Today we have _________ soup. it's made of tomatoes and _____ _________.

B : I'll take that.

A : ______ ____ ____ _ _____?

B : Cold water with ice would be fine.

A : So, that's a _______ _____ ____ ____ and a _________ _____.

B : Alright, thank you.

Dialogue 7

A : Waiter, B : Guest

B : What do you recommend for us, today?

A : Our ____ ______ is New York Sirloin steak.

I am ____ you will like it, sir.

B : Sounds good. We will have that.

A : ____ ______ ___ ___ your steak

B : Well done, please. How about you Daniel?

C : _______ ____, please.

A : How would you like ____ ________?

B : I want _______ _______.

C : I'll have french fires.

A : _____ ___ ___ __ _____ dessert now?

B : No, after meal, please.

A : Thank you.

Dialogue 8

38

A : Launderer, B : Guest

A : Laundry service.

I ____ ______ your ______, sir.

B : _____ __ __.

A : Please check it _ _ _ ______.

B : Should I pay in cash?

A : __ ___ ___, sir.

You can pay in cash or ____ __ _ so that you can ___ ____ when you _____ ___, sir.

B : Then, I'd like to sign for it.

A : No problem.

Dialogue 9

Locations and Directions

① **A** : Which room is Mr. In?

B : Let me check. Yes, he's in room 707.

A : Where can I find room 707?

B : Take the elevator on your left. ____ right when you come out of the elevator.

② **C** : Excuse me, where's the coffee shop?

D : It's on this floor. Just ______ ___ _____. You'll see it at the end of the corridor.

③ **E** : Can I buy stamps in the hotel?

F : Yes, Ma'am, at the ___ _____ on the 2nd floor.

④ **G** : I have a meeting at the conference room. Could you tell me where it is?

H : Yes, sir. It's on the 2nd floor. _____ ___ ________ the turn left and the conference suite is just on your right.

CHAPTER 4
HOTEL SERVICES–ON THE PHONE

Dialogue 1

39

A : Housekeeping, B : John Kim

A : Hello, this is housekeeping. May I help you?

B : Yes. This is John Kim in room 704.
The room is too hot.
I think the __ _________ is __ __ _____.
Could you _____ someone to __ _ __ right away?

A : I'm sorry for the inconvenience. Let me check for you. There is temperature control panel on the wall. Is it _______ _______?

B : Sure, but thermostat doesn't _____ __ _____.
I couldn't sleep well.

A : I'll send an _______ to ____ ____ __ _ right away.
_ _____ _______ ____?

B : No, that's all. Thank you.

Dialogue 2

A : Guest, B : Operator

A : Operator, did anyone call me up while I was out?

B : Yes, there was a ______ ___ from Mr. Park.

A : What did he say?

B : He said ___ ___ ___ __ when you ______.

A : Oh, I see. Thanks a lot. And I'll __ ___ for 2 hours again. I ______ _______ ___ after that. If you _______ the call could you please __ ___ ______ to come to the hotel?

B : Yes. I will.

A : OK. thank you.

Dialogue 3

40 *A : Operator, B : Heesoo Kim, C : Front Deck Clerk*

A : Good evening, operator.

B : This is Heesoo Kim in room 605.

I'd like to have a ________ ___ at 6 o'clock in the morning.

A : ____ __ ______. I'll _______ ___ to the front desk.

C : Front desk. How may I help you?

B : Can you give me a wake-up call at 6:00 o'clock in the morning?

C : May I have ____ _____ and ____ _______.

B : My name is Heesoo Kim in room 605.

C : Yes, Ms. Kim in room 605, ________ ___ at 6 o'clock in the morning.

I'll ____ ____ __ _ by myself.

Dialogue 4

A : Meejin Lee, B : Operator

A : Operator? This is Meejin Lee in room 806.
I'd like to _____ __ ________ ___ to Seoul.

B : Is it a person-to-person call?

A : Yes. The party I want to call is Choelsu Lee.

B : _____ _______ ___ ___ _____ __ ___?

A : Area code 01 and the number is 342-1456.

B : Very well, Ms. Lee. I'll ___ ___ _____ as soon as your party is __ ___ ___.

(pause)

A : Hello, Meejin Lee speaking.

B : Hello, this is operator. ____ _____ _ __ ___ ___. Go ahead.

A : Thanks.

Dialogue 5

41

A : Front Desk Clerk, B : Guest

A : Good evening, this is Pacific hotel. May I help you?

B : Could you tell me if Mrs. William is ______ in the hotel?

A : Hold on, please. I'll ______ __ ____. I'm sorry. There is no one here by that name in any other room. Maybe you have the wrong hotel.

B : I'm sorry but, can you ______ ______?

A : ____ __ ____ ____ his name?

B : That's W-I-L-L-I-A-M.

Dialogue 6

A : Clerk, B : Linda Kim

A : Swiss Hotel. May I help you?

B : This is Linda Kim calling from Korea.
Can I speak to Mr. Brown in room 545.

A : Just a moment... Hello? I'm sorry, Mr. Brown just _______ ___ of his room.

B : _____ ____ ___ ____ ______ ____ _____?

A : He _____ ___ _____ until 7 p.m.
When he ______ __ the hotel, _____ _ _____ ____ call you back?

B : ____ ______ ___ _____. Just tell him that Ms. Kim called.
He's ___ my number.

A : Very well, Ms. Kim. I'll give Mr. Brown the message.

CHAPTER 5

CHECK-OUT

Dialogue 1

42

A : Guest, B : Clerk

A : I'm checking out. Can you prepare my bill, please?

B : It's all ________ __ ___, sir.

A : Oh, good, then I'll settle it now.

B : ____ ___ ___ ______, sir?

A : I'd like to pay with Visa card. Is it Okay?

B : ________, __. ____ _ ____ __.

A : Everything looks in order. Is ______ ______ and __ ________?

B : Yes, they are __ ________ in your bill. Would you ______ ____ ____ on the bottom?

A : Oh, sure.

B : Thank you, ____ _ ____ ______ and your _____ ____. I hope you _______ ____ ____ with us.

A : If I visit here again, I'll choose your hotel again.

B : Thank you so much, sir.

Dialogue 2

A : Guest, B : Clerk

A : I'm going to ______ ___ today.
What is the check-out time?

B : 11 a.m., sir.

A : Do you ______ __ ______ ___ if I do not ______ __ _____ by 11 a.m.?

B : Yes, we do.

A : I didn't know that.
I'm _____ _ _____ my room by 11 a.m.

B : _____ ___ ___ ___ your room number?

A : Yes, room 545.

B : You ______ __ three nights, didn't you?

A : Yes, I did.
____ _____ _____ ___ ___ come to?

B : It comes to a total of $520.
____ _____ ___ ___ _ ___?

A : Do you accept traveler's check?

B : ________, __.

Dialogue 3

43

A : Clerk, B : Jeeny Lee

A : Good morning. May I help you?

B : Hi, I'm going to check out now. ___ ___ _____ ___ ___ ___?

A : May I have ____ _____ and _____ ______?

B : Jeeny Lee, 257.

A : It ______ __ $336 ma'am. ____ _____ ___ ___ __ ___?

B : I'd like to pay by Visa.

A : Would you give me your _____ ____ ___ ______, please?

B : Here you are.

A : _____ ___ ___ ___?

Here is ___ _____.

I hope you ______ ____ ____ ____ __, ma'am.

B : I really enjoyed my stay here.

A : I'm ___ ___ _ ____ ___ and we ___ ______ _ ______ ___ sometime next.

B : Thank you.

Dialogue 4

A : Guest, B : Bellman

A : I'm going to _____ now.
Would you _____ someone __ to my room 1002 for my baggage?

B : __ __ ____ _____.
(Knocking on the door) Bellman.

A : Please, come in.
Take these two baggages down to the front desk.

B : _ _____ ________ I can do for you?

A : No thanks.

References

신입전문훈련 영어교재, 대한항공.

이동희(2007). 항공실무영어, 새로미.

이향정 · 고선희 · 오선미(2009). 최신항공업무론, 새로미.

장미향 · 허선영(2005). BICS 관광영어, 대왕사.

정종훈(2002). Air Service English, 대왕사.

Inflight Announcement Manual, 아시아나항공.